Parla Möller
10/14/13

resentment
resistence
revenge

PUBLISHED BY

PSI PUBLISHING
ISBN 0-965994-4-0
ALL MATERIALS© 2008 PSI SEMINARS, L.L.C.

LIBRARY OF CONGRESS CATALOGING-IN-PUBLICATION DATA

WILLHITE, THOMAS D., 1940-1983
PATH TO LIBERTY/THOMAS WILLHITE
1. SELF-IMPROVEMENT 2. PSYCHOLOGY

PRINTED IN THE UNITED STATES OF AMERICA

PATH TO LIBERTY

by Thomas D. Willhite

Thomas and Jane Willhite, Spring 1983

This book is dedicated to

THOSE I LOVE

My family,
friends,
associates,
and
students

Nothing in this world is new...not this book... nor the paper on which it is written. The very atoms which comprise my body and yours are ancient. Though the atoms themselves are old, the arrangement, that is the way they are combined, is new. Similarly, there are no new truths. The Truth is, and always had been and always will be. I can neither add to nor take away from the truth. All I can do is to present it in a different way. Present it my way, as I understand it and as I see it applying to the NOW.

All truths are universal. I cannot teach them; no one can. You already have access to them. Instead of teaching I "educate," which means literally "to draw out". I "draw out" what is already there. This is the function of PSI – to draw out truths. PSI is not a reli-gion; therefore, it cannot be in conflict with any religious beliefs. PSI is a vehicle...a means of seeing truths...which can be used to deliver the reality of peace of mind, liberty, love and wisdom to the world of today.

The gift of being human is the ability to separate the past, present and future. The wise person distinguishes the past from the future and chooses to be here now. NOW is the key. That is what these manuscripts are about. By controlling the NOW, you control the future. By controlling the future, you control the past. Thus, each person has the ability to chart his life, to control his whole life – past, present and future – by simply controlling the NOW. Disraeli* said it simply: "Every man crucifies himself between two thieves: one the regret of yesterday and the other the fear of what tomorrow might bring." In other words, most men are living in the past or the future rather than living in the NOW. When you find a person who con-trols the NOW, you have found a leader... a leader of self.

Being a leader of self does not mean neglecting everything else. You must be aware of what you leave behind.

Think of yourself as a large ship. Have you ever seen a ship that didn't make waves? The larger the ship, the larger the waves, or wake. The wake is what is left behind. It is the past. The wake is going to affect something: it could tip over a small boat…or cause damage on shore. The law of the sea says you are responsible for your wake. So a captain of a ship is constantly watching where he is, and the effect his wake is going to have after he is gone. The law of life says you are responsible for the waves in life that you create. You are liable for your wake! A leader understands that. He makes waves and accepts the responsibility for those waves.

This manual is about leadership – personal leadership. It is definitely not a course in how to lead the masses nor a short cut to making a million dollars nor a road to fame. It is, instead, about how to take control of the NOW…all else is a side effect, a result of your taking control. To illustrate the "how to" I will need to talk of "results"…both mine and other leaders'. Keep in mind the process, for it is the process, more than the results, which is important. If you lose sight of the process, you will be like a ship that loses its bearing. Not knowing where you are, how can you know what effect your wake will have?

The only real requirement for understanding and achieving personal leadership is the ability to distinguish the NOW from the past and the future. College degrees, years of experience, even the ability to read and write are not necessary. These things are great, and you may have or desire them; but they are not essential. The Truth is simple, or it is not the Truth. Do you really think God (or that SUPREME POWER, whatever it is) would create a man so complex that only theologians or intellectuals could comprehend mankind?…or hide the Truth so deep that only a handful in the history of the world could ever understand? God is not a bigot.

The Truth is simple...so simple that every living man, woman and child can understand...or it is not the Truth.

The Truth is: you are your thoughts. You are as you know yourself to be in your heart...your soul...your being NOW. This is the basic concept – the secret of life and success. All I say or write is but an expounding on this one simple Truth. You are your thoughts.

In this letter I have given you the sum total of the entire manuscripts. I did this purposely: first, to illustrate the simplicity of the Truth and, secondly, to give you a tool to measure your own growth. After you have finished reading the manuscripts, and periodically thereafter, come back and reread this letter. The message is the same, but you will hear it differently each time.

Look within yourself now: you will see that I am with you though not present physically. I am individually with each of you as your read these manuscripts. Be with me...

Thomas D. Willhite
January 1, 1978

---

* Benjamin Disraeli (1804 – 1881), Prime Minister of England. Born Jewish in a time of anti-Semitism, he rose to the highest position in England and earned the respect of his countrymen.

TABLE OF CONTENTS

1

THE BOOK OF
BEGINNINGS

"Part of the price you must pay
for any knowledge is to discover
it for yourself."

Thomas D. Willhite

BEGINNINGS

"Every man's life is a fairy tale written by God's fingers."
~ Hans Christian Andersen

SUMMARY: This is my story, the story of my beginnings, my youth, and my years of growth. It is not all happy, nor is it all sad. It is my life. You may be surprised to find a lot of your own life in mine. Because when you get right down to it, we really are very much the same.

My name is Thomas D. Willhite. I am the founder of PSI WORLD, a nonprofit service and research corporation. PSI WORLD owns itself. It is not owned by me or anyone. I serve it as best I can.

We have another company, PSI Seminars, a profit-making corporation which teaches and markets a variety of self-improvement courses to the public, industry, business world, government and various other institutions. The PSI courses you have taken are taught by this for-profit corporation.

Voluntarily, out of its proceeds, PSI Seminars supports the nonprofit corporation. PSI Seminars is PSI WORLD's principal source of revenue at the present time. My wife and I, as well as many of our executives also give personally to PSI WORLD. This nonprofit organization does not support me or our family in any monetary way. PSI WORLD develops materials and conducts research relevant to courses taught. In addition, it sponsors numerous projects to serve mankind. There is a very small staff. Thus, nearly all of its resources go directly to produce results: creating materials, supporting an orphanage, establishing prison rehabilitation programs, energy conservation, developing new energy sources, research into human potential, and development and support of educational programs. Between these two - PSI WORLD and PSI Seminars - there is synergy. PSI Seminars offers avenues for individual growth and prosperity based on individual results, while PSI WORLD offers ways to serve humanity through giving with no thought of return. Both share the goal of peace, liberty and prosperity for mankind. One approaches the goal through the free enterprise system and individual initiative. The other by lending a helping hand where needed. This is explained now, at the very beginning, so you can better see how you and the various PSI staff members fit together. I want you to clearly understand that our lifestyle is *not* accomplished at the sacrifice of the PSI dream and cause. Rather, the PSI dream moves ahead because so many of us support that dream with our own money, effort and love. Every donation made, every hour volunteered, even every positive word spoken about PSI helps create the dream. You have helped, or you would not be reading these words. You are part of the PSI dream. Thank you.

The above paragraphs really are the end of my story. They reveal where I am now. I have wealth, power and, most importantly, liberty. I have most of the things most people would like. I did not start with them. *I created them.* I created them with my mind, with the thoughts I chose to think. I created them by conscious choice. My future, likewise, will be the result of conscious choice. To think is to create. This is the essence of our message. I use my life story as an illustration, to demonstrate the power each person holds to create their lives in the way they choose.

You might be thinking to yourself, "Well, I'm a bit too old to change a whole lot," or "I'm not the right sex or color or physical appearance to really make it big." These are excuses to avoid responsibility. You *are* the right age, color, IQ, sex and physical appearance to create an exciting, happy, successful life. You are the right being to make it big, and to make it great. *Now* you are as right as you will ever be. You always create your life as you choose, both now and in the future. Know you can have a life of liberty, like mine, if you choose. Look at my life and see your life. Look at what I did and see what you can do, *because if I can, you can.*

If I can create wealth, liberty and happiness, *you can do the same. And you can do it NOW.*

Fifteen years ago I was flat-out broke. I had lost everything and my prospects for success looked pretty grim. Even as late as eight years ago (1970), I did not own much more than the clothes on my back and a well used car.

I was born on January 10, 1940. That makes me just thirtyeight as I write these words. Somehow it seems longer ago than that, but perhaps that is only because my surroundings now are so different from then. I was born in my maternal grandmother's home, a small, old farmhouse, during a raging blizzard in southeast Oklahoma. There was no phone to call the doctor, so my dad and grandfather drove the old truck through deep snowdrifts to the nearest town. They even made it back with the doctor in time. Anyway, I arrived safely and became one more mouth to feed. Life was truly hard then. Food was scarce, jobs were all but nonexistent. Both my parents had come from large rural families of miners and sharecroppers. Both knew work early. At the age of six, my mother took over the care of younger brothers and sisters, cooking and "mothering" the little ones as they arrived. Even after she married my father at eighteen, she continued to do the weekly washing for her parents, brothers and sisters. Washing then, by the way, was done on a scrub board. In a poor family of nine children, everyone works. My dad and his twin brother were the youngest of seven children. Having been born and raised on a small farm, he also knew work well. I admire my parents for the courage and strength with which they faced hardships. He was a man who would walk eighteen miles to court a girl; she was a woman who willingly scrubbed by hand five loads of clothes a week to help her family. Somehow, in all the disadvantages and hardships, they made life meaningful and beautiful. Amid the work and poverty they found joy, laughter and spiritual strength. This is the environmentment in which I grew up.

My parents gave up farming before I was a year old, and moved to California in search of a better life. We settled in the Torrance/Redondo Beach section of Los Angeles. Here I would spend all my youth and teen years. Both my parents worked long, hard hours to make ends meet. My most vivid memories are those of being teased. They called me "Okie." I wore secondhand clothes and always felt "less than." I vividly remember one incident when my sister and I were sitting in our old car, waiting for my mother. An old man, probably a drunkard, burst out laughing when he saw us in that old jalopy. A pair of "ragamuffins," he called us. I can still feel the shame I felt then, the sense of helplessness and anger.

Of course, there were good memories, too, like the time mom did not have even a dime until payday, so I prayed for a dime for ice cream, and found one! I remember the happiness of getting a bike, even though it was used and came three weeks after Christmas. There was the thrill of getting my first car, bought and paid for with money I had earned myself.

Shortly after my eighteenth birthday, my youth ended abruptly with marriage and then the arrival of a son. I held a variety of jobs: ambulance driver, store salesman, gas jockey, anything

I could get. I had no confidence and certainly no self-esteem. I barely made it through high school only to emerge into a world where I was qualified to do nothing but menial tasks. To top it off, I moved my family into the only place I could afford, the old ramshackle house where my parents first lived when they moved from Oklahoma. I hated that place. It made me feel poor, helpless and alone. Negative thoughts welled up inside me. I had, indeed, hit the bottom, and it would be a long time until I would find the strength and knowledge to pull myself up.

Perhaps in defiance and desperation, I turned to a heavier involvement with motorcycle gangs. Drinking, smoking, violence and women became a common occurrence. This is a time I do not like to talk about and yet you need to know that I've been there. Maybe you've been there too. I was lucky enough to avoid serving time, though I probably deserved it, but I could not avoid the prison into which I had placed my mind. I was a prisoner of poverty, bad luck, circumstance and the words "I can't."

It is hard to say when the picture started to change. I tried night school and didn't make it. I tried working as a salesman in a sporting goods store, and got to be a manager. I tried car racing, and injured my back. I tried to buy and run a gas station and lost everything. I went to Bible College and was politely asked to leave after a year. My marriage fell apart. I lost custody of my three children. My life had little direction, yet somehow I was convinced that I would not live forever in poverty. I would not knuckle under and say, "That's life." I would fight and keep at it until I found a way. At this point in my life, I met a man who totally changed my way of thinking. This man was my tutor, William Penn Patrick[1]. A man who came from humble beginnings as I did, he applied many of the basic concepts taught in PSI to achieve both personal and corporate growth rarely matched in this world. Although he was controversial in many aspects, his ability to recognize and communicate the concepts helped enrich thousands of lives.

When we first met, I hated him. I looked at him and said to myself, "I'm smarter, younger and have a higher IQ. My education is about the same as his. Yet that S.O.B. has everything I want, and he did it on his own." That really made me mad. He had the things I wanted and didn't know how to get. I was jealous For many months I remained bitter and wrapped up in my own bruised ego. Finally, I was able to put those feelings aside and became determined to learn his secret. I learned his philosophy; then I lived it. I checked the validity of his philosophy in my own life.

Today, I find that I'm the one who agitates and angers people I dress expensively, fly planes, own expensive cars and live very well indeed. It is all a validation of the concept that *to think is to create*. If that's true, then should I not create the best? Why create a tent when you can create a mansion? If I am, indeed, a master of the techniques, then should I not demonstrate them? "For the tree is known by his fruits" (Matthew 12:33), said the great master; and I agree. Talk is cheap. I believe that if I am going to talk about "to think is to create," I had better produce the results. I will demonstrate the concepts so that you know for sure that you can also.

At the time I met William Penn Patrick, I was working for a large, direct-sales organization. As I grew to understand him, I started doing much better. I made money - quite a bit of money due to my way of thinking at that time. I moved up in the company

[1] For those of you who seek to know more of William Penn Patrick, you will find his story in Chapter 10 of Succeed and Grow Rich Through Persuasion by Napoleon Hill.

ny and gained responsibilities. Around me were men and women who mouthed Mr. Patrick's philosophy but did not practice it. I was confused. Why weren't they fired? I thought the higher they were, the closer to the man, the more perfect they should be. I was shocked when I discovered there was no perfection, not even in my tutor. But he understood that if a company is to grow, it must start with people where they are. Then they will either grow or change, or they will eventually leave. It is still that way. It is that way now with PSI. The PSI staff is not perfect; rather they are growing and changing. I'm certainly not perfect either. There is a lot for me to learn.

My success in sales, my rapid growth in the company, and my "perfectionist" attitude did not help me win a popularity contest. In fact, I made many enemies. The result was a scandal involving dozens of people - with me as the fall guy. I tried to get Mr. Patrick to intervene. He would not even see me. I later heard his reaction was, "Let's see how he handles this one." He knew that if a man has commitment and courage, he will fight his way out. He also knew the only way I could grow strong was to fight my own battles. If you are a leader, you may lose a battle, but you will win the war. I lost that battle but good. I crawled home and did nothing for a month.

During this period I met and later was to marry a dynamic woman from Boston: Jane Corwin. That she stood by me and supported me through these struggles was a measure of her strength, commitment and love.

Then an opportunity came, in a roundabout way from my tutor, to attend a consciousness-raising seminar taught by a company in which he had an interest. Jane and I went there together. We had never before attended anything like that. It seemed freaky and far out. In fact, I slept through at least half of the class. I knew my tutor also wanted me to attend the instructor's class for this seminar (which, in my opinion, had done absolutely nothing for me). I did not understand why, but I did attend. Two weeks later I still did not understand what the whole thing was about, or why I was there. "The reason why you are there is not important for you to know now," was the message I got. That was typical of messages from my tutor. He never sent a kind word, never a word of encouragement, never a stroke. He understood that I needed more than strokes. I needed challenge, for only through confrontation and challenge could I obtain rapid growth. So every time I saw him, he challenged me; he dared me, and he nailed me to the wall. He nailed me on my personal life, my divorce and remarriage, my spiritual understanding and my business practices. *He nailed me on the concepts with the concepts.*

Two weeks after I had completed the instructor's training, I put together, totally by myself, a class of twenty and taught that class according to the set plan. The lectures were short - I didn't have much to say about the outlined topics of reincarnation and psychic phenomena - and the breaks were long. Sunday night I went home and became very, very ill. Gradually, I understood that I had violated the principles. I had stolen from those people. I had given them meaningless lectures. They had come in feeling "less than," and I had sent them out feeling "better than." That day I made the commitment to myself that I would never teach that class again.

When I saw my tutor, I told him what I have just told you. He responded that he felt there was a great deal of good in the class, but could understand how I felt also. "What would you do to improve that class?" he asked. I suggested some changes, mainly adding his philosophy into the lectures, then tailoring the meditation cycles to the philosophy and the realistic problems of the students. I also suggested including some kind of test to show people where they really were in understanding the philosophy. He said, "That sounds good." Then he asked, "Do you believe in the philosophy?"

I said, "Yeah."

"Well, what do you do with the concept 'if you don't like something, change it'"? I was nailed to the wall again. "Be sure you understand that one, so when you write it, you write it properly. If you know a better, more positive way that is synergistic and 'win-win' for everybody, it is your responsibility to change it. Now, be clear, this has nothing to do with your likes or dislikes, your ego, your programs or personal tastes. This concept is much deeper than that. It has to do with what is right It has to do with what is synergistic."

I understood and said I would try to put together a new course, and I assumed from the way the conversation had gone that I had my tutor's full backing and support. I went off on top of the world, thinking I had it made. I taught workshops, trying a few new ideas; and in all my spare time I'd work on the new class. Finally, after about six months, I was ready to try it out. I presented the idea to the management and was very politely told where to go. How could I, an unknown, uneducated, "un-everything," have the audacity to suggest an entirely new class? They wouldn't consider trying it, so I ran back to my tutor, asking for his intervention. "Nope," he said, "I am not about to endorse it. If it is Truth, it will survive; and if it is not, then it won't. To be proven, that class needs to meet resistance, and I am going to help you by giving you resistance. I won't even acknowledge I know anything about it." I was crestfallen, to say the least. So it was back to pleading and bargaining until, finally, I got permission to test the class.

And test it I did. I went to the lowest sales area in the direct sales company for which I had previously worked and gathered thirty "bust-outs." These were thirty of the lowest sales people. If the class was to work, it had to work for those who needed it most. I had to show those people who were at the very bottom the "how to" of getting to the top. If they understood and were motivated to apply the concepts and actually produced the results in their own lives, then the class could be termed a success. And it worked. The class was a tremendous success. Now nobody could deny the validity of either the concepts or the class. I thought.

But management didn't see it that way. Sometimes you can do everything right, and they still do not like it. Instead of letting me continue in the test area and expand from there, management assigned me a new territory out in the boondocks. Nevertheless, the class succeeded there too! Then there was another assignment to a failing area and the struggle to build up again. It seemed that just when things started going well, they squashed me. Later, I would learn that my class and I were producing the most students and the biggest successes in the entire company. Why did they resist the class so? Why would they fail to acknowledge my successes? Why? I don't know. Not all things can be explained by logic and reason!

In June of 1973, William Penn Patrick was killed in an accident. I mourned his loss, but I did not and do not miss him. How could I? He's with me all the time. Using my levels and workshop, everything continues: conferences, meetings, talking back and forth daily still take place, only not on the physical plane. People ask, "Is this some kind of talking to spirits?" I don't know. Does it really matter? From using my levels and workshop, I gain strength, peace and insights and that's what is important to me.

With the death of my tutor, most of the ties that held me to the company I was working for were then broken. We were still going in different directions. It was time for a parting. To have proselytized other employees, or stirred up the field by publicizing my resignation would have been a violation of the principles. That I could not do. I could not take, even when I had been taken from so many times. By taking, I knew I would lose and fail. You cannot steal from a thief; you will lose just as much as if you steal from an honest man. So I quietly left.

Three weeks later, PSI was formed. Over the dining room table in my home, PSI became a reality. It consisted of my wife and me, $200 capital, and a dream of the way people could live and the way a company could be. I began building and teaching ing classes while Jane handled the business end. Later, she would become a fantastic instructor in her own right. But, in the meantime she was my chief writer, organizer and doer of odd jobs, not to mention also being a wife and mother. We were a synergistic team. Very soon others joined with us. PSI was on its way!

We did pretty well the first year. We did very well the second, even better the third, and the fourth year was incredible. Since then, the growth has been phenomenal. But what pleases me most is not the number of employees PSI now claims, but a simple little thing: Many of the people who started with us are still here. Through all the ups and downs, and we have had our share, they have been able to perceive the Truth in the concepts and apply it to their lives. PSI is a better way of life. It works. I get so excited when I think about it that I want to shout, "IT WORKS!"

In the first few years every cent Jane and I made was ploughed back into the corporation. This was the only way to keep up with PSI's growth and to assure that PSI WORLD, the nonprofit corporation, could stand on its own. That is now achieved. PSI WORLD owns and governs itself. It has outside investments, interests, activities and continues to work synergistically with PSI Inc. PSI Inc. continues to give a portion of everything it makes, a portion of every class fee, to PSI WORLD for the furthering of peace, prosperity and liberty for mankind. As PSI Inc. grew and prospered over the years, gradually our lifestyle became gracious. Very, very gracious. We have gained liberty: access to travel, freedom to do the work I choose, greater areas for creativity and lack of worry. I do not worry about losing everything I have, even the corporations, because I know that if I lost it all today, I would just build it again. *Liberty is first and most of all, a state of mind.* Of course we do have problems and challenges – without these PSI could not grow.

Two PSI WORLD projects have special meaning for me. These are the prison project and the orphanage. First, the prison.

The prison program began with the idea that all men can know freedom and liberty if only they can free their minds. To give freedom to men in prison would seem impossible to many. We chose to see it as a challenge. The target of the challenge was Hawaii State Prison, one of the most violent, hard-core prisons in the country. This prison made the newspapers almost every week with violence and corruption. In fact, it became so bad that the National Guard had to be brought in to control the situation Here was a real test of the concepts and the class. It was also an opportunity to pay back a debt. I owe my tutor a lot and the only way to pay him back is to serve others as he served me, to free others from their mental prison bonds.

I can really relate to those men in prison. I played a pretty violent game when I was younger. I did a lot of wrong things and things of which I am not proud. Those men in prison got caught, and I didn't. They are serving time in a physical prison. I served years and years in a mental prison. I had to free myself from mental bonds and so must they.

PSI began in Hawaii State Prison in the spring of 1976. It began with a class of the twenty-four toughest men the prison could offer. They're still tough! Just try to overlook a concept, and they'll nail you to the wall! From the first class developed a second, then a third—after that, advanced classes. To date, over two hundred inmates have participated in one or more of the PSI programs. The results are history, printed in newspapers, in legislative committee reports and in testimonials. Hawaii State Prison has changed. Gone is most of the violence. In its place is communication Gone is the frustration and hostility, replaced by self-esteem, commitment and direction. This may be hard to conceive, yet it exists today. You can see it for yourself. The prison superintendent Antone Olim, expressed it this way: "PSI has had one of the most positive effects on Hawaii State Prison that I have seen in my thirty-six years at the Institution, including the last ten years as superintendent." The men of the prison program are very special to me. They are truly my brothers. I love them very much.

It is my desire and hope that the prison program can be expanded into other prisons, juvenile homes and correctional institutions. There is tremendous interest, but the problem is funding. So far, PSI WORLD has had to carry the burden alone, completely financing the expenses for all the prison classes, instructors' fees, travel expenses and materials. Requests have been made for state and federal funding, but it has not yet been forthcoming. At times it reminds me of that situation I had years ago when management wouldn't support us. But in time the prison program will expand. I can see it clearly in my mind, and because I can see it, I know it will happen. "To think is to create" is a Truth.

The prison program has a special message, even if you never step inside a prison. It has significance for each person in PSI. That significance is this: if these men who have touched the bottom can pull themselves up, you can. If those who are confined can find liberty, then you can. *If they can, you can. Do it!*

The second of the PSI WORLD projects, which is dear to my heart, is the Casa Hogar Alegre Orphanage. The orphanage is not owned, run, or in any way controlled by PSI WORLD. We just support it by sending as much money and materials as we can. The orphanage is in a rural and mountainous area of Mexico and is run by American missionaries. They are beautiful people with a beautiful dream to take all abandoned and mistreated children of the world and turn them into healthy, happy, self-sufficient young people. If you ever get a chance to visit the orphanage, you will see the dream in action. Many of the children are special: Down Syndromed, mentally handicapped, physically handicapped, or emotionally disturbed. They are special because they need special love, care and devotion. I am proud to support such work, and you can be proud too, because whether or not you know it, every time you have supported PSI classes or activities, every time you recommended PSI to a friend, you have helped with the orphanage project, with the prison project and with every PSI WORLD project.

Today (in 1978), as I write these words, PSI classes are taught in major cities on both East and West Coasts and in Hawaii. Classes are also taught in Canada under the name of Willhite Success Seminars. (Due to a name conflict with another company, we are unable to use the PSI name in Canada.) Soon, other areas of the world will be opening PSI classes. Already, PSI materials have been translated into Spanish, German and Japanese. New PSI classes are being developed, and old ones are being upgraded. It is an exciting and thrilling time and there is more to come. The story of PSI has just begun!

Time is, indeed, relative. For my first thirty years I barely lived; I mostly existed. I had everything going against me, yet now I have a great degree of liberty and I have everything going for me. In just a few short years, my life turned around. I have lived more in the past few years than most men live in a lifetime. It is not the quantity of years that counts, but the quality of the years that counts. Will this be a quality year for you? It will be for me.

I want you to think about something that I had to learn the long and hard way. For the first half year or so, I put my tutor on a pedestal. Everything he did I saw as perfect. I tried to be like him in every way. I almost made a god of him. Then, one day, I saw he was just another man. He put his pants on one leg at a time. So, I totally blew him right off that pedestal. I became disillusioned, negative and sometimes even hostile. My production (I was in direct sales at the time) dropped drastically. After a few weeks of being down, I started thinking of what the man did right, and he did a tremendous amount right. I blocked the negative things from my mind because they did not matter. The mistakes did not matter. It was the right things that mattered. I asked him once why he let these mistakes be known, why he didn't cover them up. "Wouldn't you be more effective," I asked, "if you had a more clean-cut image?"

"I am who I am," he responded, "and I am not creating an image just for you."

I had to take a look at that and come to grips with it. I was forced to do some wrestling with myself, to think about my image. What should it be or not be? Finally, I came to realize who I was and where I was. Next I looked at where I was versus where I could be. My life gained perspective. With perspective came insight. I realized that I must always continue to grow and change. Now I find myself changing and becoming more positive every day. I just keep working on myself, and I do not worry about what has approval out there. I do not try to hide my mistakes. It was just as wrong to put my tutor on a pedestal as it was to downgrade him for his mistakes and for personal habits which I disliked. So now I try to see other people as they are and for the good they do. This was a hard lesson I had to learn.

There is a price for all things. There is a price for every PSI class and a price for every success. I have never had anything free in my life. Not ever! Nor have you. Wisdom is being able to determine what the price is when it comes. Sometimes the prices are absolutely astounding. If you read carefully this chapter, my life story, you will see that I have paid some very high prices. It is between the lines and behind the successes. I have not told you everything explicitly. Part of the price you must pay for any knowledge is to discover it for yourself. You must learn your own lessons and make your own mistakes. You must pay your own prices, and . . .

YOU MUST CREATE YOUR OWN LIFE STORY.

2

THE BOOK OF ATTITUDE

"If you don't like the way
you feel, change it. It is
your responsibility."

Thomas D. Willhite

ATTITUDE

*"It would be no great overstatement of the truth if we said that
mental attitude is EVERYTHING."*
~ Napoleon Hill

*SUMMARY: Attitude is the key to all behavior…the key to action. In this
book we look at how attitudes are formed and changed. What does it mean
to take responsibility for our attitude? How do we create positive attitude
habits? What is the price you must pay for success? These are the questions
we seek to answer.*

Life need not be a forty-hour-per-week job and television in
the evenings. Life does not have to be just enough money to
pay the bills. It can to be more than a two-week vacation once a
year. For those who understand the rules, life is fabulous. It can
be exactly what you want it to be. *There are no limits*, except those
you put on yourself. The world is yours. When I was a kid, I used
to think the greatest thing in the world would be to have meat
every night, instead of maybe once a week, and to always have
new clothes, not someone's hand-me-downs. Life was hard; it was
work. And when I got older, I lost jobs, couldn't pay bills and
went through a broken marriage. I even managed to flunk out of
college. Not surprisingly, I had a constant attitude of poverty and
failure. It was not until my late twenties that I began to understand
and take charge of my life. To do this, *I had to be willing to change
and control my attitude*. The rest was easier after that.

At the outset we should be very clear on one point: You
don't have to have a bad attitude to get a better one. All too often
we resist a change because we assume change means that we are
faulty somehow, which hurts our self-image. So, to protect that

self-image, we resist suggestions of change. Ask the man on the street about change, he will likely say, "I don't need to change - my spouse does - or the children - or the boss does...but not me." Why not change you? Why not do more and be more? If you agree it might be a good thing to extend your limits, then you have already begun to change your attitude for the better.

Within each of us lie values. Symbolically speaking, they lie at the center of our being. Love, a passion for life, honor, good health, and peace of mind are some of the positive and natural values we all respect. They are positive growth ideals which exist in our deepest core as Truths. And not far away, these values are surrounded by programs. Programs are automatic responses. They are similar to putting a plane on autopilot. Press the button and the automatic control mechanism takes over. Basically, programs are intended to help us achieve the values we hold. At birth we have about 2,000 programs designed for instinct, living, functioning ing and positive growth. But, soon after birth, we begin to adopt other programs based on our immediate environment and the society in which we live. Usually we have an unconscious acceptance of those programs which we perceive as being necessary for survival. Whether or not these programs actually reflect our values, or represent Truth is immaterial. It is our perception at the time we accept a program that matters.

A child who is led to believe by word or action that he is stupid will develop a program of failure. A child who is led to believe he has worth will develop a program of success.

By our middle teens we have adopted most of our major life programs. That is to say, we are already functioning on autopilot. In light of this, it's easy to see how you might end up with a lot of negative programs that are working contrary to your values.

Take a little boy who is told, "Men don't cry." Does he stop and say, "No, you're wrong"? Of course not. He thinks instead, "This big person, whom I love and want to be like, says 'men don't cry.' So I better not cry if I want this grownup's approval." The little boy buys the program. And it doesn't matter that the big person may be unhappy or lonely, because the child doesn't perceive, or understand, that kind of unhappiness and loneliness.

The development of programs is not limited to childhood. Any self concept accepted, even if based merely on a casual comment, can be the foundation of a program.

Surrounding the programs, we have attitudes. Attitudes are the way we feel. They are the feeling sides of programs. Someone comes along and pushes one of our program buttons and a feeling erupts. It may be positive: happiness and joy; or it may be negative: hate and envy.

So at the core are our values, surrounded by our programs and habits, which in turn are encircled by our attitudes, positive or negative - all of which, at times, can be pretty well hidden, even from us. But on the surface, enclosing it all and observable to everyone, is our *behavior*.

Behavior is simply the way we act. Facial expressions, hand gestures, phrases and words we say are some of the ingredients of behavior. Generally, behavior is a reflection of attitude. You feel good and there is a smile on your face; you say pleasant things and people know you are happy by this behavior. Conversely, if you feel rotten, everyone knows that too: downcast eyes, listless movements, a tense or drawn look, a sigh. Consistency between behavior and attitude is normal. Generally, *we behave the way we feel.*

Occasionally, it is necessary to control behavior, that is, to behave in a way which is inconsistent with our attitude or feelings. On that first date, most people try to be charming or witty, at least pleasant; no matter how bad they may feel. A business person, meeting for the first time with a million-dollar account, will be alert and attentive to the client, regardless of a pounding headache. We've all experienced things like this, perhaps not realizing there is a very important discovery here: *we have the ability to control our behavior despite our attitude.* We do not have to behave the way we feel. The conscious mind chooses how to act. Now, the amazing thing is that by controlling the behavior, we can control the attitude. We can actually choose how we want to feel by choosing how we behave. *We feel the way we behave.* So if you don't like the way you feel, then change your behavior.

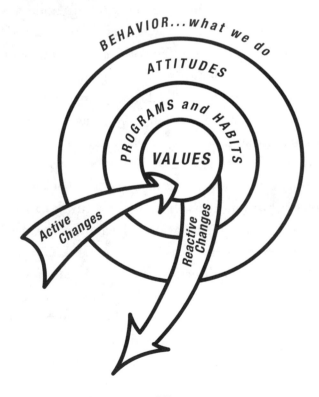

Attitude Affects Behavior; Behavior Affects Attitude.

This statement implies there are two ways to change an attitude or feeling that you do not like, as illustrated in the drawing on page 23. The first is to work from the inside of the circle outward: values, programs, attitude, to behavior. To change an attitude this way, you would start with programs and say, "I don't like that program; it doesn't represent my values. I don't like the way I feel when that program gets activated." Then you have to consciously choose to change the program and to eliminate certain troublesome attitudes when they come up. "I choose to feel better - I choose to feel more positive - I choose to feel successful." By deciding to think positively and selecting a winning attitude, you will start to feel like a winner and then behave like one. As this is done over and over again, your behavior will, indeed, change. You will begin to act like a happy, successful person. Others will begin to see you in a new way. The process of changing programs and attitudes by controlling your thinking can be a lengthy one. "There are days when I have a hard time controlling my thinking, much as I want to," people say. "I'm really trying, but those negative tive thoughts just keep popping in when I am not looking." That is the way it seems as you change thoughts. It will take a while and you might not know in advance exactly what new behaviors will emerge; but change will happen. I think of this as the "reactive way" of changing behavior. Behavior is changed as a result of changes in programs and attitudes.

Going the other direction is easier. I may have trouble controlling my thinking some days, but I know I can control my behavior. This is the "active way" of taking control. Controlling behavior is going at the circles from the other direction: from the outside in. And when I choose my behavior, the miraculous thing is that my attitude will then change to reflect it. If I keep at the new behavior and new attitude for a while, lo and behold, a new program has replaced the old. My autopilot has a new set of directions, ones I have consciously chosen. Isn't this the easier way of the two? It certainly is for me.

Would you like to experience this way, the "outside-in" way of changing right now? It is easy to do. I just want you to jump up from your chair, arms waving in the air, and shout, "I'M EXCITED!" Be sure to get all the motion, all the thrill, of a kid jumping for joy at the thought of going to Disneyland for the first time. Do this exercise now. I dare you to really do it, right now! And I double dare you to do it if you are in a public place.

How do you feel? Can you sense the energy, the excitement? If you got up each morning for 30 days and did this exercise, the changes in your life would be phenomenal! So I challenge you to do exactly that. Do this exercise every day for one month and experience the power under your control. "Aha," you say, "it can't do all that much." Then I challenge you to prove me wrong! Put everything you have into this exercise for one month, then write and tell me I am wrong. It works; it really works. I've done it.

If you don't like the way you feel, change it. It is your responsibility.

On the next page there is a chart, which illustrates the relationship between specific attitudes and specific behaviors. Let us suppose you often feel frustration. It could be in your work or at home. Perhaps you don't know why, you just feel that feeling. Locate "frustration" on the feeling side of the chart. Next, look across to the behavior side. Most likely, you are exhibiting one of those behaviors listed across from frustration. Are you hating yourself, putting yourself down, being envious of someone else?

ATTITUDE AND BEHAVIOR CHART

NEGATIVE ATTITUDES RESULT IN NEGATIVE BEHAVIORS

ATTITUDES OR FEELINGS	RESULTING BEHAVIORS
Depression	Self-pity, self-centered actions
Anxiety	Resentment, revengeful actions
Guilt	Anger, displays of temper
Remorse	Defiance, disregard of others
Fear	False pride, boasting
Dissatisfaction	Greed, stealing and lying
Irritability	Illness, insomnia
Tension	Envy, coveting others' things
Loneliness	Impatience, intolerance of others
Withdrawl	Blaming others, avoiding responsibility
Failure	Isolation, no communication
Indifference	Worry, nervouseness
Frustration	Not trusting others
Confusion	Scattered thinking, no goals

- -

POSITIVE ATTITUDES RESULT IN POSITIVE BEHAVIORS

Happiness	Rich, full life
Tolerance	Energy
Humility	Joyful living
Satisfaction	Laughter, smiling
Patience	Love, giving and receiving
Faith	Showing compassion
Warmth	Expressing gratitude
Love	Concern for others
Optimism	Generosity
Responsiveness	Honesty
Usefulness	Service
Service	Direction in life
Acceptance	Recognition of self and others

Maybe you are exhibiting dissatisfaction with your environment and all those around you? One of those behaviors will fit. Find it. Now you have a choice. You can change the behavior, or you can change the feeling. You can change from inside out or outside in. Either way, you will shift from the top of the chart to the bottom - to the positive, happy attitudes. The responsibility is yours. You will find that you no longer need crutches. Crutches are like cigarettes, coffee, computer games, or whatever you use to "get you through" the day. Do it yourself. Stay off your crutches. Think of all the money you can save! Think about how great it feels to be in control, total control of this thing we call attitude.

You are responsible for you. Assuming a responsibility means changing a wrong into a right. In other words, if the way you feel is not right, then assuming responsibility means changing it. Responsibility means "to take care of." Let me give you an example of the meaning of responsibility. When we were getting PSI started, a business venture was proposed. One of the executives brought an idea to us which looked pretty good. He had it well laid out, and most of the staff thought it could work. I had some reservations but felt these could be my own negative programs. So I set my personal feelings aside and said to him, "I believe in you. You make it go." In other words, I gave him the authorization *and the responsibility* to go ahead. The program was launched, and 11 weeks later, $70,000 net had already been lost.

At the next executive meeting, I was sitting at the conference table when he sat down and said, "Well, I really laid an egg, and a square one at that. *But* I accept the responsibility. I really want you to know that I take total responsibility."

I said, "That's incredible. This is the first time I've ever had an executive who would accept the responsibility. Where's the check?"

"What check?" he said.

"The check for the $70,000."

"Oh, I didn't mean that," he explained

I said, "Wait a minute, you said you accepted the responsibility That means if something is wrong, you make it right. 'Making this right' means giving me the $70,000 that was lost."

"I didn't mean quite that."

"Oh, you mean that if there is going to be anyone badmouthed, anyone gets lip service, you accept that responsibility."

"Yeah."

"That doesn't count."

Who was really accepting the responsibility? *I* was. Because I saw it as my $70,000, and it was my responsibility to come up with that $70,000 to make it right.

Take this story and relate it to your life, personal, family and business. Understand what the word *responsibility* means. Throughout all our writings and teachings, we keep saying, *accept the responsibility for your life*, which includes your attitude, your behavior, your success and for where you are right now.

A lot of young people say to me, "I'm 13, or 16, and I'm able to accept responsibility for myself." Are they? It seems to me they're talking about authority, not responsibility. Authority means the right to make a decision, the right to do something, the right to act. Taking authority is simply making a decision regardless of the outcome. On the other hand, to take responsibility is to guarantee the outcome of your actions. In a negative situation, responsibility means to make it positive, to make it better.

Anytime there is an imbalance between authority and responsibility, there is destruction and failure. When you have a balance, generally you will have success. The most striking imbalance between authority and responsibility during the 20th century was the Nazi regime. Haven't you ever wondered how Hitler got so many thousands of people to commit so many atrocities against their fellow human beings? He did it by giving his followers the authority and then, in effect, said they didn't have to take the responsibility. "This is your job; you have the authority to kill those people with poisonous gas. The responsibility is the State's." And so the followers did those terrible things *without accepting the responsibility*. If you are in business, watch out for that balance. Those who have too much authority and not enough responsibility are not productive and are often destructive. They usually accept authority eagerly, yet resist accepting responsibility.

Obviously, there should always be at least as much responsibility as authority. When that is balanced, you are moving in the direction of success. Maturity is accepting the responsibility and totally understanding what responsibility means. So when we say, *accept the responsibility for your attitude*, we mean (1) become aware of how you think and how you feel; and (2) if there is any negativity, or if it is simply not as you want to feel then change it to make it right.

There is one attitude that is almost intolerable for positive, productive people to be around. It is poisonous both to the individual with the attitude and to everyone with whom he or she comes in contact. That attitude is *complacency* - that attitude of being neither hot nor cold, neither for nor against, neither here nor there. Surely you know someone who fits this description: Mr. and Mrs. John T. Average, age around 35, 2.3 children, no particular political leanings, vaguely interested in local affairs. They're middle income, middle of the road, and totally *dead* emotionally. They are dead to life, not buried yet, but dead nonetheless. Do you know what it takes to get John T. Average off his complacent butt? It takes a full-scale atomic blast - which may come in the form of a massive coronary, a serious automobile accident, the loss of a dear one, or the destruction of all his material goods. It is far easier to turn a hater into a lover than to move the complacent. Why? Because the complacent person is afraid of change, afraid to take a risk. He has so much insecurity and fear that he is stuck dead center. On the other hand, the hater is actually moving - but in the wrong direction. All that's needed is redirection. If you have ever ridden a motorcycle, you'll understand what we mean. Going along at a good clip, it is very easy to change direction even if that new direction is uphill, because you are already moving and have momentum. However, when you are stopped cold and attempt to push that heavy bike up even a slight hill, it's a hard, hot, dirty job.

Most people have an attitude of tolerance about their work. They put up with it but do not really like it. It is just a means of keeping food on the table and clothes on their backs. That attitude is not quite, but almost, as bad as complacency. Who is responsible for your attitude and where you are? *You are!*

The person who really wants to get ahead in life, to be great, or to have great happiness, is the person who learns to work and to enjoy every aspect of it. These are people who see themselves enjoying their jobs or careers, actually having fun with them. They make work a pleasure by choosing to see the excitement in it. They get turned on about the ordinary agonies and frustrations because they realize the role these play in their lives: they are stepping stones towards their goals. Such people are not schemers; they don't want to wiggle out of work and try for every shortcut. They can be honest with themselves, knowing hard work is a fundamental law of success. And it is primarily an attitude.

I have known a number of people who were brilliant and total failures. They felt they were too smart for work. Sometimes they were lazy and refused to apply their abilities, and almost always they were searching for a shortcut, a "get-rich-instantly powder" to sprinkle on themselves. There is none.

If you want happiness and success, but you don't like work or making decisions or getting down into the dingy, dark corner of details, then you can choose to start liking it. Start wanting to go to work a little early - and leave a little late. Start getting engrossed in whatever it is you must do. Start looking for ways to do it better and you will create an attitude of liking your work. You will become a success.

Attitude programs, or habits or automatic response patterns, are performed under the direction of the subconscious, rather than the conscious mind. Most of our daily physical activities fall in this category. Writing a letter, eating a piece of toast, even just getting out of bed in the morning are all habit actions. The muscular movements are under the direction of the subconscious. We do it automatically. As a child, through practice and repetition of these movements, we became proficient. The skill became easier and easier. As this happened, we gradually became less and less conscious of the details of movement until we reached the point where there was no conscious effort at all. The movement had become a habit. The task of performing a given activity had been transferred from the conscious to the subconscious. We were still totally in control, but at a different level of mind. Now the same thing has to happen with the new attitudes we choose to develop. They must move from being a conscious effort to a subconscious habit.

Those actions/habits are completed with great efficiency, maximum performance and with minimum conscious attention. I'm aware of the truth of this when I fly. My Cherokee 6 is equipped with many instruments and gauges, more than the average small plane. After years of flying, I have come to *sense* when it is necessary to make adjustments in fuel mixture, prop speed, angle of pitch, and all the other factors which a pilot controls. Think of yourself as you drive a car, and you will understand what I mean. The "sense" is nothing more than the subconscious processing the input of information, such as engine sound, climb rate, feel of the wheel, etc. Of course, this is very frustrating to a beginning pilot. Picture yourself flying with me. You would experience a bewildering amount of input because your conscious mind would be required to do everything. If I were compelled to put out the same amount of conscious effort to every detail of flying as I did when I first started to fly, I would not now be flying. Subconscious habits are necessary for proficiency, speed and mental rest. *Conscious attention requires tremendous mental energy.* What has this to do with developing new positive attitudes? It means that, in the beginning, it will take a lot of mental energy - a total conscious effort - to create the new attitudes in your life. However, through repetition, these attitudes will soon move into the realm of the subconscious. Then they will no longer require conscious energy; they will be attitude habits.

A word of caution: the subconscious is just as apt to pick up a bad habit as it is a good one. Thus, if you let your consciousness dwell on frustrations, worries and failure, these are the attitude habits you will pick up. Part of the function of the conscious mind is to supervise the subconscious. You are responsible for its actions whether or not you are aware of them, and whether or not you are willing to admit it!

Since building a habit is the process of educating the subconscious, and the easiest way to do that is to change our behavior, here are some useful steps:

(1) Begin with concentration. Your conscious mind must give attention to every aspect of the desired new result. What does it look like, what does it feel like, what behaviors does it cause and what reactions does it get? The conscious mind must be totally

familiar with the result you want so that the subconscious mind will receive clear directions. Could my subconscious mind work with precision while flying if I had allowed my consciousness in the beginning to be sloppy? Of course not. The more conscious attention given to the development of the desired attitude or behavior, the faster and deeper it will go into the subconscious.

(2) Recognize that it is your intention for your subconscious to take over for your consciousness and thereby create an attitude habit. This can be done through visualization and affirmations. I like to think of my subconscious as my personal helper. I address it and treat it like an independent person: "Hey, Subconscious! I am learning to fly, and I want it done right, with accuracy and precision and, of course, with a minimum of energy. You watch me for a while until you get the hang of it. Soon I'll ask you to do it, and I expect you to do an even better job than I can." Does this approach work? Try it, and then answer for yourself.

(3) Trust your subconscious. Once you have turned over a task to your subconscious, having followed steps 1 and 2 above, let the subconscious do its work. Your conscious task is to examine the results, not meddle in the details of how the subconscious does its work. If you turn over a task to a trusted friend, do you question every move he makes? Certainly not. Your subconscious is your trusted friend. Treat it as such. One of my colleagues is an excellent tennis player. However, I have a sure method to throw off her game. I simply ask her how she serves, or how she does a backhand. In her attempt to analyze her subconscious movements, she disrupts the flow and ease. The following verse expresses this well:

The centipede was happy quite,
Until the toad, for fun, said,
'Pray, which leg comes after which?'

This wrought his mind to such a pitch,
He lay distracted in the ditch –
Considering how to run.

These three steps - concentration, recognition and trust - are the keys to building habits, whether they are physical habits or attitude habits. Some of the attitude habits we suggest building might go like this:

I do well everything I do, big or small.

I finish all that I start.

I tackle the difficult tasks first.

I expect good and truth from everyone until shown otherwise.

I give acknowledgement to the achievement of those around me.

I get a laugh out of life every day.

I willingly pay the price.

Take time, now, to make two lists. First, a list of the habits you already have that you like and, second, a list of habits you want to create.

The last attitude listed above, that of "being willing to pay the price," is a very special one. We have chosen it as the last topic of this book on attitude because it is so important. If you are to be successful, you must create this attitude and make it a habit.

What does it mean "to pay the price"? The answer is not simple, for the price may come in many forms. Furthermore, paying the price is not a one-time action; it is a continual process. So unless "paying the price" becomes a habit, you will usually fall short of your goals.

The easiest price to pay is that of hard work. Most men and women of achievement have had to put in long hours, combined with persistent and often strenuous effort. The rancher who gets up at 5:00 a.m. and works until dark is paying the price of hard work. So is the Olympic champion who practices eight hours a day besides holding down a regular job.

Another price is that of self-denial. Self-denial is the giving up of a present pleasure for a longed-for future pleasure. The family who will cut out luxuries in order to save money for a down payment on a home of their own is paying such a price. Notice how much harder it is to pay the price of self-denial than to pay the price of hard work. Gladly will a child pick up their toys for a chocolate-chip cookie. How about exchanging that cookie for a hot fudge sundae some two days from now? No way. The child has not learned to pay the price of self-denial. For example, look at the person (perhaps the one in the mirror) who desires to lose weight and can't, who desires to stop smoking and can't. It is likely they are not yet willing to pay the price of self-denial.

By far, the hardest price to pay is that of "relinquishing desires." This is the true meaning of "paying the price," for it is the ultimate cost. Relinquishing desires means willingly giving up those aspirations which prevent or hinder obtaining a higher objective. The person with two sweethearts who chooses one and lets the other pass by "pays the price." Many business executives have chosen success over family and paid a heavy price for it. Others have chosen work over recreation and paid the price in terms of health. Clearly, the heaviest prices are when one desire is relinquished for another.

"Paying the price" does not mean we must give up everything for our main desire. That would be a great injury in fact, for it would restrict our interest and attention too severely. It does mean that we must relinquish conflicting desires, or modify the desires so there is no conflict. We must pay the price by giving up all that interferes with the attainment of a goal. It's a good idea to give up the image of loafing in the sun all day, if you're planning to run a million-dollar corporation. You would not have to give up an image of yourself owning yachts, swimming pools and the like, because this image works toward your goal, not in conflict with it. The key to keeping the price from being too heavy - to avoid paying for success with a heart attack - is to transform conflicting desires into those that support the direction you are going. The person who wants to be a success and keep a close relationship with his or her family can do so by involving the family in the business and the business with the family. Business trips can be family outings. The family can learn to pitch in and make the business successful. The conflicting desires no longer conflict. The price to pay has changed.

But never think you can escape paying the price. It is there, whether or not you acknowledge it at that moment. Usually the greater the object you desire to obtain, the greater the price. A Mercedes costs more than a Hyundai. It may be that the end result is not worth the price one is asked to pay. In such cases, willingly give up that goal. Personally, I will not pay the price of separation from my family in order to obtain a larger income. There are other roads to success.

When I am asked to pay a price, I ask myself, "Is this end result really worth what I must give up to obtain it? Will I in the end be truly happier, stronger, a better individual?" When the answer is an unqualified yes, then I willingly pay the price.

Said the gods to man, "Take what thou wilt - but pay for it."

 *3* ❧

THE BOOK OF DESIRE

"Don't let the sun set without taking some strides down the road to your goal."

Thomas D. Willhite

DESIRE

"A human being with a settled purpose must accomplish it; nothing can resist a will which will stake even existence upon its fulfillment."
~ Benjamin Disraeli

SUMMARY: Desire is that emotion which turns thoughts into actual creations. In this book, you will see that desire is a learned emotion, based on imagery and repetition. Furthermore, it is a positive emotion working toward what you perceive as good. Within this book lies the key to all success and achievement. The understanding and control of desire is the very basis of every leader -- positive or negative -- throughout history.

All things begin with thoughts. The chair you are sitting on was first a thought in someone's mind. This book began as a thought. The actions you are now taking to become a leader - reading these manuscripts, attending PSI Seminars - were first thoughts and then, when desire was added, a reality. So it is with everything in your life. Nothing, not a piece of food, or a telephone call, or a conversation, comes into your experience except by way of a thought *first*. The phrase, "thoughts are things," is a Truth. Perhaps it would be even clearer to say, "Thoughts are the only things." The understanding of this concept is a major key to success, whether that success is in the form of riches, leadership, health or spiritual awareness. These manuscripts are all about understanding and putting into use this single concept. If one truly understood this one thing, none of these teachings would be necessary. That is how powerful it is.

This concept may be seen in action in my own experience. My thoughts actually ended up affecting thousands of people. I refer to the very beginning of PSI back in 1973. At that time the whole of PSI was but a single idea: liberty for mankind. I pondered along this line for some time; general, nebulous thoughts, which were more like hopes and wishes. But in the summer of 1973, following the death of my tutor, I realized it was now time for action. I began by turning the hopes and wishes into a more defined vision. In my mind I conceived an organization dedicated to peace in our lifetime. I saw classes teaching people how to do this. I saw the need for buildings and for expansion of those buildings. I saw a network of people surrounding the world, and lighting up that world. I heard the concepts explained in many languages, by people of all nationalities and races. All this was done in my mind alone. At that time, there were no outward manifestations. I worked only with my wife, Jane, who enthusiastically shared the vision as a true co-creator. We had no financial support, other than our own earnings. Through visualizing our concept over and over again, with all the details, an intense desire began to grow within us. Note, I said that the intensity of the desire *grew*. It did not start that way, but rather was the result of the visualizing and imagining.

With the desire also came the faith that this idea could be created. So we started to plan how we would organize the classes, and what to include. During this time our minds quite naturally gravitated toward books and people who were compatible with our thoughts. Consequently, all the specialized knowledge we needed to put our plans into action was available. By December, our thoughts had grown to include about a dozen people. Then disaster struck and those who had been with me left. But our thoughts, our visual images, continued. We refused to let them go despite all outward appearances. By February, all those who had left returned. They brought with them an even stronger commitment and greater energy. Thus, an apparent failure had turned into a significant forward thrust. The desire that burned within us now burned within several others.

Exactly twenty months from when we had begun to specifically formulate our thoughts, we moved into Casa Montana on High Valley Ranch, a multi-million-dollar complex in the beautiful coastal range of Northern California. We were able to do this despite having lost $70,000 on a project that did not work out. Today, High Valley Ranch serves as the world headquarters for PSI. The nebulous thoughts that were shaped into a powerful concept became a vital reality in only a few years. Today it encompasses hundreds of thousands, including you, for you are now beginning the exploration of that thought.

Through this example I hope you will glimpse the significant role of desire in the process of becoming a leader in your own success. Desire is an emotion. In fact, it is the emotion by which thoughts are turned into things. It is the underlying drive that enables you to face the negatives and apparent failures on your chosen path. The desire for liberty, and for giving other people the opportunity to have liberty, is the one thing that kept us going during the disappointments, the failures and the bad times. And so it must be for you if you are going to turn your thoughts into reality.

Let's look more closely at this emotion called desire, specifically at how to generate it. Actually, there are two types of desire that most people experience. There is the natural or instinctive desire. For example, the desire to survive, have a family, love, sex, togetherness and acceptance. The second type of desire is the created desire. Created desires would include the desire for a large home, for wealth, for a new car, for a plane, for designer clothes, etc. Created desires are conceived in the mind. The more we envision the thing we want and the more we dwell on the positive aspects and benefits of this thing, the greater our desire for it will become.

Desire is developed by dwelling on the positive, not the negative. Suppose you are a young person about to finish high school. You have just started to think about college. Most of the thoughts are probably about the fun: the parties, the new friends, living away from home, and the freedom to select classes. Intellectually, you will acknowledge the need to do homework, take tests and go through ups and downs. But you do not admit these seeming negatives on the emotional level. You only taste the diploma, the liberty it will give you, the companionship and newfound knowledge. As you think along these lines, within you the desire to attend college will build. The stronger that desire, the more obstacles you will be able to overcome to achieve your goal. Perhaps you will have to work to earn money for college, or you'll need to improve your grades, or increase entrance-exam scores. But always pictured in the front of your mind are the positive benefits of higher education. I'm convinced that most students drop out of college not from lack of ability, or the difficulty of the work, but rather from disillusionment and the corresponding destruction of their desire.

Desire is a positive thing. A person who desires much is usually a person who dreams positively. The opposite is a person whose dreams are mostly negative. They generate fears of rejection failure, shame and loss. If our college aspirant starts to think about all the papers, the hard work, the tests, the competition, and the unfairness in grading, the result will be a feeling that "I'm not good enough" or "I won't make it." Carried to the extreme this negative dreamer might develop a strong desire to avoid seeking further schooling. We have said desire is positive; so how is "not seeking further schooling" positive? It is necessary to look to the end result for the student. The student desires to escape the perceived dangers of college work, so avoiding it actually seems positive, in his or her mind.

Having a strong desire for success does not mean you'll feel great all the time. No matter how enlightened most anyone becomes, they will not be positive all the time. The pendulum must swing back and forth. The only alternative is to sit in neutral, which is precisely what most people do. By cutting off all their negative feelings, they experience neither the negative nor the positive. They are unfeeling. They don't like rejection so they don't go out on a limb. They avoid insecurity by dodging risk. They run from loneliness by staying in their own sheltered world. In short, they have a disease called complacency. Theodore Roosevelt described this well when he said, "I pity the mediocre man who lives in the gray twilight of existence without knowing the agony of defeat, or the thrill of victory."

It is easier to turn a negative leader positive, or turn a hater into a lover, than it is to move the complacent off dead center. For this reason, a true leader will respect a negative leader or even a hater more than the mediocre. If you feel at this point that your life has been tending to the mediocre, do not despair. The purpose of PSI is to get your pendulum swinging. If you follow directions by actively participating in all the exercises, it will simply happen.

Here is an easy exercise to demonstrate that desire can actually be created. To experience the desire building, you must be willing to spend the next ten minutes at this task. It should be enjoyable, because desire is positive.

We think of vacations as being fun, producing good feelings. So right now conceive of the greatest holiday of a lifetime. Pick someplace on the earth that you picture as being the perfect vacation spot.

Write it down. Now visualize the place. See exactly what it is like with you there: the colors, the excitement, and the sounds of this specific place. Spend as much time as you need to actually do this.

The moment you started to visualize your ideal vacation spot, your feelings probably began to change. So no matter how negative or disappointed you were before, your feelings have begun to change right now. They are not the same as they were a moment ago. Your subconscious mind does not know the difference between fact and fantasy and makes no distinction between the two, which is why you can wake up from a dream in a sweat or screaming. Only the conscious mind can make the distinction between illusion and reality To the subconscious mind, your ideal vacation is a reality.

To a large degree we are our subconscious minds. So to create a positive desire, we need to begin our mental conditioning there. That is, we need to change our thought processes. By controlling them, we can change the reality of what we are at the moment to a different reality. It can be done right now using your dream vacation. However, we will need a checkpoint. So write down how you feel right now. What is reality for you at this moment?

Reality is only in the now. Thus, what you wrote down is past and there is already a new now. We must measure reality in seconds, not days or years. Change the reality for you in the now simply by making a decision.

Now write down when you want to take your vacation. Make it realistic within your present time commitments. Look at your destination and the time frame. Are you really serious? If you are, then right now make the commitment to yourself to go to such and such a place on the date you wrote down. The reality of what was two minutes ago is no longer the reality of now. By your commitment, your emotions have begun to change. The decision is causing your subconscious mind to change. Now, if you are really serious about that commitment, you will immediately call or write a travel agency near your home and have them send you all the flight and tour information they have on your planned destination. As you hang up the phone or finish the letter, you will feel different. What do you feel?

Let's project this exercise a little further into the future. When you receive all the travel information, you will look at it and decide on a specific tour. Call the travel agent and make the reservations. At what point in time do you start to feel good? At what point do you start to feel excited? When you get there? After you have gone? No, the point at which you start to feel good is the moment you conceive of your vacation in the mind. And that feeling intensifies as you make the decisions leading to the actual trip. The moment you conceive it in the mind and hold the image is the point at which you start to build desire - desire that will result in your taking that trip.

You put some money aside. You notice clothes that would be appropriate to your destination. Your reality has changed, and yet *you're not there*. You begin to count down the days. It is coming closer and closer. You schedule the time off. You buy the last minute stuff. And still you are not there. The reality is that *you are continuing to do the same things you always do*. Life is going on the same way. You are not on your vacation, yet.

But finally the day comes. You go to the airport and in reality it is still the same. *But* your feelings are all different! Your desire is so powerful that you have manifested what you wanted and, in fact, are already reaping what you sowed. And still you are not there, yet you are experiencing the joy, the thrill and the excitement.

Finally, you arrive.

At what point in time did you start feeling good? Before you got on the plane? Before you got the tickets? You began feeling good the moment you made the decision to go in the direction you wanted to go. You had to make the decision and the commitment to create the reality you wanted.

When you create in your mind what you want to be and make that decision, your whole being begins to change.

This is desire and how it is created.

To have a burning, consuming desire, it must be for something. This something I will call your definite main goal. Notice carefully the three words I use: "definite," meaning specific; "main," indicating the most important; and "goal," implying an end result. Each of the three words is equally important and a critical element for success. Each word is necessary in order for a burning desire to be created.

Whatever it is you want you can have, provided:

(1) You can state specifically what it is.

(2) You want it so badly that it becomes a consuming desire in your life.

(3) You have faith in your ability to achieve it.

(4) You are persistent in your efforts.

(5) You are willing to pay the price for success, whatever that price may be.

Read the above statement again. In one sentence, it is the formula for success. Be sure you understand it, and commit it to memory. If you have not yet achieved the degree of success you desire, the problem lies in one of the five conditions, probably the first one. Studies indicate that 95% of the people in the United States do not have a definite main goal in life. They exist on a variety of "wants" and "would likes." It is little wonder that this majority will be at the same place ten years from now as they are today. So let us begin by finding out what your definite main goal is.

What specifically do you want to achieve in your life?

Before you go any further, stop and write down your answer to this question, in as much detail as you can.

If your answer is something along the lines of "to be rich" or "to help make the world a better place" or "to spread peace throughout the world," then you are being about as definite as a two-year-old when asked to describe the universe. "Peace," "love" and "happiness" are great, but they are not a definite main goal. They are not the stuff upon which burning desires can be built.

The problem with defining your definite main goal is that you have many desires, hopes and aspirations, some of which are probably conflicting. To begin to make sense out of the picture, make three lists: "Things I Want," "Things I Want To Become" and "Things I Want To Do." Put your strong desires and dreams down, regardless of whether or not you feel you can obtain them and regardless of how ridiculous they may seem. It may be that by continuing to work through these manuscripts, you will suddenly think of new desires. Return to this page, and add them to the lists. For these are desires you might have suppressed, feeling they are unattainable. Listen carefully as your subconscious speaks to you.

At this point, your list may seem like a hodgepodge of wants and likes. As you proceed, you will shift, arrange and eliminate various goals. That is the process of arriving at your definite main goal. Begin by objectively reviewing your lists, striking out the insignificant or temporary desires. Combine those that are essentially the same. Make a decision between those that are conflicting. After you have done this, your list should be substantially smaller, consisting only of those goals which are highly important to you and which will add great meaning to your life. You may now wish to pause for a while and give your subconscious time to do what it will with this input. If you do so, by the end of twenty-four hours you will find that you clearly know which of the remaining goals on your list are the most significant for you.

As a general rule, each goal which remains on your list should meet these criteria: "that it brings pleasure or eliminates pain for you or for someone dear to you, without hurting or hindering in any way another person." If a goal cannot meet these criteria, it is not worthy of you. It must be eliminated or reworked. For if the success of your goal means the injury of another, then your success will be a hollow one; and the price will be terrible. *You get back exactly what you give.*

The goals that remain on your list must be in harmony with each other. If there is a conflict between two goals, one must be eliminated. "A house divided against itself cannot stand" (Matthew 12:25). It is not possible to achieve two conflicting goals, nor is it possible to build desire in two directions at once.

If you have done the things we have described so far, you have probably arrived at between one and five significant goals. If you have more than five, then I suggest you repeat the screening process. And do it again and again, until only those goals for which you can develop a burning desire and commitment remain.

Now we will begin working with each goal separately. Start by writing a clear, concise statement of that goal. *Be specific.* If you want to own your own business, then what type of business is it? How many employees? Where is it located? What are the gross annual sales? How much profit will you make? Who are your customers? Will you buy the business or create it? When? What service or product will you provide? The more precise the statement of your definite main goal is, the better your chances of achieving it.

A definite main goal commands respect. Think of some great leaders - positive or negative - Churchill, Hitler, Jesus, Mohammed, and Buddha. Is there any question in your mind as to their definite main goal? Their followers knew their goal and supported it. If you intend to be a leader of yourself, or of others, you must know the direction which will take you to your *definite main goal.*

Imagine with me for a moment. In my mind I have created an ultramodern, newfangled think machine. It works like this: You attach a set of three electrodes to your head, turn it on, and the machine will create exactly whatever it is that you are visualizing. It creates instantly. Do not worry about how it does this, it just does. If you are thinking about a banana cream pie, it produces a banana cream pie. The same is true for a house, car, or horse, whatever you come up with. Let's say you want, really want, a Mercedes convertible In my mind I would see the end product, the beautiful, gleaming body, the color, the upholstery and maybe some of the extras, like the CD player. However, if the machine kicked out exactly what I visualized, I would not have what I want. I would have just a shell: exactly what I saw. There would be no engine, no working parts, nothing to make the car run, because I did not visualize any of these things. However, if I want the machine to produce a totally functioning Mercedes convertible, all I have to do is see all of these parts in detail and see how they relate and function together.

It is the same for you. You must see your definite main goal as an end product, and you must also see all the facets, all the details and workings that make up that end product. *What you see is what you create. Thoughts are things!*

If you feel like you're struggling with innumerable, unanswerable detail questions, know that I have been there also. Earlier, when I described going to my tutor and telling him I could not possibly teach a certain class because it made me ill, it was totally in violation of the principles. His response was, "So do something about it." Was he not saying, "Form your own *definite main goal*"? I needed to be specific about what I wanted to teach and exactly how it was to appear. When I got that part figured out, I asked his permission to teach this new class I had now created. Surprisingly, his answer was *no*. I could not have his permission. In my ignorance, I stated, "That means I cannot teach it." And his response was, "No." It did not mean that either. He could neither give nor withhold permission. *Only I could do that.* So it is with your definite main goal: *Nobody can give you permission to do it*! No one will answer the questions for you. You must answer the questions for yourself. The decision to "do" is yours alone.

Suppose you plan one or more aspects of your definite main goal incorrectly. You select a product to sell that does not sell. Perhaps you've located your tofu and sprout store in Itsybitsyville, North Dakota, only to discover the community has no interest in tofu. What is the result? The result is you know something that does not work. And you will be able to modify your definite main goal to make it even more specific. In this case you might try chicken-fried steak on the menu, or, better yet, relocate to a tofu-friendly city. But if you don't do anything, and make no decision, then you'll know absolutely nothing more. Knowing what does not work is almost as good as knowing what does work. *You can't lose by making a decision.* Edison discovered tungsten would work as the filament for an electric light bulb only after trying thousands of substances that did not work. But every one of them gave him a better chance to find that certain combination which would work.

By this point, you will have a definite main goal in mind, one which is written down and specific. In order to get to that goal in the shortest possible time, you will need some sort of a road map.

First, start by listing all the parts that make up your goal, both in terms of necessary skills and the physical things you need to possess. Dig deep, for this is a very difficult task. Suppose this business you wish to set up is one in which you will design, make and sell handcrafted products. Here are some questions you will have to ask yourself:

SKILL QUESTIONS	PHYSICAL QUESTIONS
• Do I have the skill to make my product? • Do I have the speed, or mass-production ability, to make this a profitable idea? • Do I have the ability to sell my product? • Do I have the skill to manage others who will work for me? • Do I have the skill to manage the cash flow, keep accurate books and organize the mechanics of this business? • Do I have the stamina to give it my all? • Am I willing to accept the responsibility for whatever may happen?	• Do I have a place to do my work? • Do I have all the tools I need? • Do I have a source of supply for materials? • Do I have an outlet for my finished product? • Do I have the resources to pay my bills while I get started? • Do I have a way to advertise and get my product known? • Do I have a way of getting feedback on what I am producing? • Do I have a way of getting my product to my customers?

As you concentrate on your goal, many more questions will appear. The answers will form the stepping stones on your road to success. Arrange these stones so that you have a specific plan and time frame in which you shall acquire the needed skills, or physical things, which lead toward your definite main goal. With each step you take, you will find your desire for that goal becoming more all-consuming. Each step is a decision reaffirming your commitment. Remember the example of your dream vacation. Each step - deciding on the place, getting brochures, making reservations - increased the desire until you experienced the joy and the excitement of the trip even before you left. Now do it with your definite main goal. Fortunately, everyone does this process of deciding on a goal and building desire correctly some of the time - by accident. The classic case is that of a young man dating a girl. It is natural to be successful. Tutors and manuals are not required, because all the knowledge you need is within.

Thoughts are Things

Desire Starts

Now let's get back to our young man. Sometime between the ages of six to 18 he is going to create his perfect woman. He will think of this woman and will see in his mind her image. All he will have at this point is her image. As time goes along, he will see in greater detail this image. On a scale of 1 to 10, she will be a 10. He will see and know all about her. Next, he will start to see himself with her, doing things together. This is the starting point of desire, actually

Faith Builds

the starting point of all achievement. The next thing that comes is faith. Faith builds through the visualization of being together. He begins to believe in the reality of what can be. For the subconscious mind, the thoughts are the seed - the desire, the fertilizer - and faith is what grows! So now he has faith that someday

Organized Plans

she will come. He starts looking for her. Everywhere he looks for her... east, west. He starts planning specifically how he can meet her, where they will meet. Through imagination he sees the meeting, how it will go. Before the first date, he plans the proper dress and the proper place. Everything is set like clockwork.

Persistence

Then he makes the decision: I'm going to marry her. Maybe she says

Mastermind

"no." He keeps trying. Finally she says "yes." Together now they have a conscious agreement that they will get married. He has an emotional commitment to the wedding. They have that chemistry going for them. They have created a Mastermind that will cause his goal to become a reality. Do you have any doubt they will get married, even if his parents oppose? Even if he is black and she is white? Even if they are citizens of different countries with different languages?

Can you see this young man has gone through the entire process of being successful, naturally? In fact, he may do it many times!

It's natural. However, what is socially acceptable is not necessarily natural. Our social standards have often gotten us into a lot of trouble, by forcing us away from being natural.

It is natural to be successful!!

Most of us just hope and wish for something. We are not definite like the young man above. If you had a handful of wishes and a handful of mud, of which would you have the most? It is very important that you understand this point. Wishing and hoping are not desire. Desire is a very definite, precise image, a specific goal that you hold in your mind. In the summer of 1973, I had precise images in my mind. And today they are reality. It was only a matter of time. A measure of success is how quickly one can change thoughts into reality.

Everyone correctly follows the process for being successful some of the time. John T. Average does it accidentally. It just happens. This time it worked. He neither knows nor understands why it has worked. He is what I call an *Unconscious Competent.* Jonathan Spectacular, on the other hand, knows the rules and laws of success. He plays his life accordingly. He knows the results ahead of time and, in fact, plans those results. There is no other difference between John and Jonathan, neither in intellect, background, sex, or race. Those are just John T. Average's justifications, his excuses.

But if you are sincerely involved in this work and committed to success, *there are no more excuses.* Not even the excuse that you haven't finished these manuscripts. All that you need in order to be the *Conscious Competent* you already have *right now*. But this is exciting news, something to get really enthusiastic about!

Enthusiasm is that special quality that makes things happen. I think of it as the wind that whips the flames of desire into a burning inferno. It's the excitement you feel and express when you have faith in your ability to realize your desires. Remember when you have been enthusiastic, how much easier it was to get things done? Time flew, obstacles vanished, or could be overcome, and it was so much easier to communicate. Did you ever notice how your enthusiasm was transmitted to those around you? I do not know of anything more contagious than enthusiasm. Put a high school cheerleader in a class on Friday before a football game, and you will know exactly what I mean. Now suppose the teacher, to calm down the class, gives a pop quiz or test. Oops, all that enthusiasm simply dries up. How much more, I wonder, would students learn if that teacher had used some enthusiasm in the lesson? Cheers for adjectives and adverbs? Why not?

Enthusiasm is a state of mind, an emotion, <u>which you control</u>.

By control, I mean you can create it. If you want to be enthusiastic right now, this very second, you can create it. To start, just think about the work or service you like to do best. Can you feel a change, maybe a smile on your face? Now take that positive feeling, and transfer it to your definite main goal. Sense the feeling you will have when your goal is achieved.

Right now make a list of all the positive, good things you'll have or do when your goal is a reality. If there is someone with you now, whom you trust, share your list with him or her.

When you've finished, check your feelings. Are they lightening up? "A little," you say, "but I don't have the capital to start the new business I'm dreaming about, or the right college degrees. So how can I be really enthusiastic?"

First, remember that *no one controls your mind but you*. No one can prevent you from formulating your definite main goal, or can stop you from becoming enthusiastic about it. This is a fact.

Don't let the sun set without taking some strides down the road to your goal.

After even a few steps you will become enthusiastic, and it won't be long before you get there. My assistant is one of the most enthusiastic, energetic people I know. I asked her how she kept up her enthusiasm. "Why, it's easy," she said. "I just love what I am doing. I want to master all these (PSI) principles, and I can't think of a better place to do that. Each day I just get closer, and that's exciting!" She is striding down her road every day. How about you?

I have a challenge for you. How enthusiastic can you be tomorrow? Can you make the first person you see smile? Can you get someone else excited; maybe turn a whole town on? A country? The world? Where is the limit?

The Charter to PSI WORLD reads as follows:

"Authorized to do business in any state in the United States and in any country or nation of the world or anywhere in the universe."

Your definite main goal begins with a set of thoughts, thoughts you control. Desire is an emotion, which you both create and control. Enthusiasm is a state of mind also subject to your control. Desire plus enthusiasm is the pulsating force to create things from thought.

Thoughts are the only things.

4

THE BOOK OF CONSCIOUSNESS

"The creativity of the
subconscious is unlimited."

Thomas D. Willhite

CONSCIOUSNESS

"You are greater than you know." ~ An ancient aphorism

SUMMARY: Consciousness is all of your awareness of the moment, plus all that you have ever known or experienced, plus all that you don't even know that you know. Conscious-subconscious-super-conscious; id-ego-superego...these are but the terms we use to describe the elusive substance of our non-physical being. In this book we explore the meaning of the words "I AM."

"Who am I?" I can think of no task more frustrating and perplexing than to ponder this question. Most of us can conceive ourselves as being more than our physical bodies. Likewise, we are more than our emotions. When we put our bodies and emotions aside for a moment, there is still something beyond those things. Maybe it's our consciousness. Yet we exist in the sleep state often without consciousness. So the question remains, *"Who am I?"* It seems unfair that something so simple to ask can be so hard to answer. In this book we will look at the three levels of consciousness and how each functions. Once they are understood, we become able to direct, indeed create, all that we experience. Thus, the knowledge of these levels, Conscious, Subconscious, Super-conscious, is the key to success, whatever that may be for you. And perhaps, through this process, we will find the answer to the question, *"Who am I?"*

The most familiar of the three levels is the conscious level. It is the ordinary state of mind when you are awake. You are at your conscious level as you read these words, as you eat or do your daily chores. Many people in the world think this level is all there is. In fact, it is only a very small part of your being. The conscious level of your mind has two main functions: (1) it directs your attention, and (2) gives orders to the other levels. In other words, the conscious level is the CEO who says, "Take notice. This is exactly what I want done." Thus, all that you create, every plan you make, every goal you set, begins under the direction of conscious effort. In fact, it begins with attention.

From the numerous sights, sounds, smells and sensations that surround you every moment, you select those which fit into the pattern of your attention at that moment. Seated in a busy restaurant, you may choose to hear the banging and clatter of the dishes from the kitchen, or you may concentrate on the words of your companion. In each case, the other sounds are relegated to the fringe of your consciousness. They exist only as a part of the background noise. So it is when listening to a speaker or reading a book. We tend to be more attentive to those ideas which already fit in with our thinking. Perhaps you have experienced this: you have a new interest, such as flying. Suddenly, you will begin to notice articles in the paper or a comment on TV or will hear someone mention something related to flying. Notice how your whole world has become interested in flying. Has the world changed? No, there is probably the same proportion of references to flying in the paper and on TV as always; only now your attention has a different focus. It is accurate to say we hear exactly what we want to hear and perceive what we want to perceive.

To learn the laws of attention, watch a professional magician. He can keep your eyes on one hand while the other skillfully and often openly performs the deception. Pickpockets are equally skilled in this practice, so are parents (the fastest way to get my daughter over a skinned knee is to shift her attention elsewhere).

Most people in this world let their attention run in a random fashion. They notice the loudest noise, see the biggest object, listen to the side of the question that supports their belief and practically ignore the other side. They do step 2 after step 1, and step 3 after 2, and so on down the line. Their attention follows the path of least resistance. But it does not have to be that way. *The conscious mind controls attention, not the other way around.* If you choose, right now, you can put down these manuscripts and turn your attention elsewhere. You can choose to read the last page of these manuscripts first. You can choose to see the enjoyable side of your work. You can choose to keep your attention on the positive traits of your mate. You can choose to see an event as funny, or humiliating. The conscious mind directs the attention, and directs it specifically to those points it wants to see.

The second major function of the conscious mind is to give orders. It is the conscious mind that says, "Get out of bed," "Lift that book," "Put a smile on your face," "Look successful." The conscious mind is the supervisor who directs the work; it does not do the work. If you doubt me, just try to pick up a pencil by consciously directing each muscle individually. Very frankly, I do not even know which muscle starts, yet I can consciously give the order to "pick up the pencil." On the other side, you do not do anything without the direction of the conscious mind. No amount of wishing gets you out of bed. You can want to and know you should when the alarm goes off and you know you ought to, but only when the conscious mind actually gives the specific order: "*Get out of bed,*" do the muscles all coordinate to make it reality.

Just as with attention, most people's minds do not pay much heed to the orders they give. "Clean your plate, even if you are not hungry." "Go ahead and do it. Who cares if it hurts tomorrow?"

"Slap the child when she talks back. Never mind that it didn't feel good when you were a child." "I'll give you something to cry about!" *Most people's orders follow the path of habit.* Again, it does not have to be that way. Choose to skip that dessert. Give the order to be ready on time. Decide to talk it out rather than lose your temper. The conscious mind gives the orders that result in actions. Or it chooses not to give an order, which is simply a different kind of order. "Stand up for your rights!" is an order. So is, "Don't stand up for your rights!" The conscious mind always gives the orders.

The subconscious is the workhorse of the mind, and it is a giant compared to the conscious mind. It controls most of the functions of the physical body, as well as being the seat of our memory, emotions, habit patterns and much of our thinking and creativity. It is on the job awake or asleep, regardless of what is holding the conscious mind's attention. The subconscious mind is the source of power, the tireless force behind our being. Thus, to change life, to create a new you, you must be willing to look at and work with the subconscious.

The subconscious has four major functional areas: (1) programs. (2) memory, (3) emotion and (4) creativity. The knowledge, mental activities and processes related to these areas, by and large, function outside the conscious level. Only as we direct our attention to a specific area do we become aware of it. Pause and listen to your heartbeat. The control of your heartbeat is in the subconscious and this is the way it should be. If your conscious attention were required for every detail of movement and function in your body, there would be no time for anything else. Thus, the subconscious must always remain chiefly *sub*-conscious. The key to working with the subconscious is to selectively direct the conscious mind to areas of the subconscious which you desire to change. For example, suppose for the moment that it is desirable or necessary to increase your heart rate. First, you would direct your attention to your heartbeat. Then, you would give it directions to increase, through visualization or affirmations. Try it. See yourself racing in the Grand Prix or running in the surf of Waikiki, or dancing to the beat of an African drum, or simply repeat rapidly, "Beat faster, faster, faster, *faster*!" Now pause and check. Is your heart beating faster? If you really got into that exercise, it will be. You have used your conscious mind, through attention and giving directions, to affect processes under the control of the subconscious. Let us now briefly look at the four areas mentioned above.

PROGRAMS: In this area we include the vital processes of the body and habit patterns, both physical and mental. That covers a lot. Many people feel that the body automatically runs itself, which is only partially true. As we saw above, these vital processes, that are normally taken for granted, can be, and frequently are, altered by conscious thought. To this area we could also add the natural healing forces of the body. There is little argument today, even in medical circles, that mental states radically affect the physical body. Hence, a number of authorities hold the point of view that all diseases, at least in the conception stage, are the result of disturbances in the emotional nature, that is, disturbances in the subconscious, either real or fancied. Then, it is but one step further to the conclusion that the clearing up of disturbances *at the subconscious level* will allow natural healing forces to work and thus restore health.

Other programs in the subconscious realm include habit patterns, which were mentioned at the end of the *Book of Attitude*. Just like the physical programs, these can function either positively or negatively for the individual. Unfortunately, the subconscious does not make a distinction between beneficial and destructive. It simply accepts and translates into a habit that which comes to it repeatedly. Many a smoker and social drinker has discovered that if they *repeat any action many times*, it will become a habit, and the conscious *will learn to like it*. Think back, if you are a smoker, to the very first time you smoked anything. Was it pleasant? How did it become pleasant? With repetition. The same applies to emotional or reactionary habits. Think of a person who reacts negatively to every suggestion you make. That is a habit. It likely began in the past when negativity served them in some way, made them feel safe, or even powerful. But the behavior has persisted far beyond its usefulness.

MEMORY: The subconscious is the storehouse of the memory. In fact, many psychologists now believe that the subconscious stores all sensations that come into the subconscious through the five senses, no matter how subtle or silent they may be. Also stored with the memory of senses are remembrances of reactions and emotions stirred by the experience. Persons who have had a near-death experience frequently recount long-forgotten events in minute detail. But perhaps even more amazing is the cross-indexing of the memory. One can recall incidents according to time, place, who was there, feelings, what was said, what was done. And all of that is done *automatically.* Our memory banks are more complete and better cross-referenced than the best data base in the world. However, there is also a way of putting memories in an area called "forgotten." A failure to remember is not a passive action. Forgetting is an active process. It is done on purpose. This was one of Freud's major discoveries: forgetting is an active process used to protect the individual from painful experiences.

Thus, *you remember what and who you want to remember.*
Generally, when you leave a seminar or meeting, you carry with
you a variety of recollections. A most interesting experiment is to
go back through notes or tapes and discover what you chose to
forget, and why.

EMOTIONS: Emotions and feelings come from the
subconscious. Usually they appear in response to a conscious
stimulus. Since they are not the result of a conscious thinking
process, emotions often seem baffling and confusing. "I don't know
why I feel that way; I just do." "I can't help the way I feel." Such
statements are familiar to most of us. The conscious stimulus has
unknowingly triggered an emotional memory, a feeling which
had been stored away. If that feeling was generated by a memory
one chose to forget, then there is no conscious recollection of
why that feeling arose. Many modern psychological treatments
are simply processes of matching up feelings with memories and
uncovering memories placed in the "forgotten" file.

Generally, it is the negative emotions that give people problems.
These are the ones we do not like and try to avoid. There
are really only two basic negative emotions: ANGER and FEAR.
The ancient Buddhists called anger the "burning passion" and
fear the "freezing passion." Although both destroy, they do so by
different methods. All the other negative emotions are a combination
of these two. Jealousy: the burning desire to punish combined
bined with a fear of loss. Inferiority: the fear of not being good
enough. Shame: a burning anger at self. Greed, hate, malice all
burn. Passive aggression, cowardice and blaming all freeze. Each
of these emotions includes pain, fear, resentment, and a grudge,
a desire to escape or avoid the cause. When a negative emotion
arises, somehow, either in the present or in a past memory, the

self-respect has been injured. For the young child who sees the world as centering on himself, there are many emotional "hurts," both real and imagined. It is not the incident, even in the case of a very unpleasant experience, but the emotional impact which is the "hurt." Thus, the adult, looking at an emotional hurt of childhood, can use his adult perspective to re-evaluate both the incident itself and the emotional impact. This is the key for dealing with negative emotions.

CREATIVITY: From the subconscious springs creativity. I discovered this some years back, mostly by accident. I was working on a problem I could not solve and finally gave up in frustration. The next day, while cutting the lawn, the answer just popped into my head. This has happened more than once. So after a while, whenever I had a problem and no answer, I would give that problem to my subconscious. Of course, I didn't call it that. I generally referred to it as "Hey, you." I would say, "Hey, you, I have this problem. The solution must include this and this and I need the answer by the day after tomorrow, so please be ready." Sure enough, the answer would be there. And not only the answer but all the details as well. I don't worry about how the subconscious gets the answers. I simply use the results. Many great artists and thinkers have explained their genius in the same way. Albert Einstein said thoughts would just "float" in. And Mozart heard the aria of the quartet of "The Magic Flute" while playing billiards. Robert Louis Stevenson dreamed the story of "Dr. Jekyll and Mr. Hyde." In the morning, he merely copied it down. Richard Bach awakened one night and heard the first half of the story "Jonathan Livingston Seagull." Two years later he woke up and heard the second half. *The creativity of the subconscious is unlimited.*

Most people never really experience their creativity. They run on old programs or follow the "normal" way of doing things. Creativity is not limited to the artistic community. It is a way to live life. Every activity can become a creative experience. Have you ever had "animal pancakes?" Those are pancakes poured in the shape of cows, cats, sea monsters and giraffes. My daughter and I had them this morning. Or how about a game of checkers on the tile floor? Ever celebrated a sunrise, or toasted a moonset? Kids live creative lives and it doesn't have to change as we grow up. I have a very dear friend who makes it a point to do something she has never done before every day of her life. She is one of the most excited, creative and delightful people I have the pleasure of knowing. If you want to experience your own creativity and the excitement it can build in your life, just try her recipe for a week. Every day for a week, do something new, something you have never done before. I will bet in one week's time your life will change.

If the subconscious controls programs, memory, emotions and creativity and the conscious controls attention and the doing of things, then what is left for the super-conscious? The super-conscious is the source of inspiration, intuition, wisdom and power. Some call it universal knowledge, divine power, God. Because it operates through the subconscious and is seldom directly in our conscious attention, it may seem mysterious or unexplainable. The processes of the conscious mind do not apply at this level because the super-conscious operates "beyond" ordinary reason. I have often felt the influence of a protective power; you might call it a guardian angel, a spirit friend, a kindly genius, or patron saint. Certainly there are times when the super-conscious is apparent to me; however, I am not usually aware of its presence. But this does not diminish its power and influence. *Lack of awareness does not mean lack of existence.* Just as with the subconscious, by directing attention to the super-conscious one may become aware of its operation.

In the super-conscious is the unity of all things. Everything is known. There are no secrets. A mother senses the injury of her child. Telepathy, clairvoyance, psychokinesis, clairaudience are the processes of the super-conscious. Also rooted in the super-conscious are the basic assumptions of our own existence: space and time. Both are relative. A microscopic animal might experience its total lifetime in a matter of minutes. Does it have a less vivid experience than a tree that may survive thousands of years?

There's an old joke about a man speaking with God. The man asks, "Is a million years to me just a minute to you?"

God answers, "Yes, my child."

"And a million dollars to me would be only a penny to you?"

"That is true."

"Will you give me a million dollars?"

"Sure," says God, "just a minute."

Can you imagine a different order of beings for which a year is but a second? For them a century would pass in a little over a minute and a half. We say a person "thinks in a flash," but perhaps he is only more in tune with the super-conscious. *To think is to create*, and how fast I am able to create that which I think is a measure of awareness.

Actually, the three levels of consciousness are not separate, but one. We refer to this as the *Trinity of Consciousness*. Your consciousness consists of only that which you are aware of at the moment. Yet when you are asked to recall the events of yesterday, these recollections rise from the subconscious level to the conscious level. So where is the line between conscious and subconscious? There is none. Nor is there a line between the subconscious and the super-conscious. Everything is known.

The Trinity of Consciousness is not a new concept. The Egyptians spoke of "KA," the subconscious; and of the "body mind," the conscious mind. The early Christians translated the concept to the "Blessed Trinity": the Father, the Son and the Holy Spirit. Freud saw it as the ego, superego and the id. The table below illustrates some of the many ways this concept has reached mankind. The years to come will give us even more, until that time when man can understand and be all that he is capable of being.

Trinity Of Consciousness

Date	What it's called			Date
PSI Seminars	Conscious Mind	Subconscious Mind	Superconscious	1970's
Isis Religion (ancient Egypt)	Body/Mind	Ka	Ba	6000 to 2000 B.C.
Christian Church	Son	Holy Spirit	Father	20 A.D. to present
	Mind	Heart	Soul (Spirit)	
Freud	Ego	Super Ego	Id	1885 to 1940
Jung	Mind	Personal Unconsicous	Collective Unconsicous	1900 to 1960
Kahunas	Lower Self	Middle Self	Higher Self	400 A.D. to present
Buddhist Philosophy	Material Form (Rupa)	Mental (Nama)	The Truth (Nirvana)	Second Millennium to present
Shinto	Man/Ancestry	Magohoro	Kami	2nd or 3rd century B.C. to present

There is a fundamental thought process which is extremely powerful. We all use it, knowingly or not, and it dictates the quality of our lives. It is the I AM concept. I became aware of it as a young man, and I've continued to study it daily ever since.

Like everyone else in our neighborhood, I was "normal," as opposed to "natural," which means good, or as it should be. Everyone felt "less than" and "worthless" as though life had no meaning. I felt that way, and I had difficulty coping with experiences. Almost every day my buttons would get pushed. Small things would trigger emotional reactions, which, seemingly, I could not control. For example, in church I would hear that the teacher Jesus said, in effect, "All things I have done you can do also," and "I have come as a pattern unto mankind." He was saying, "All those things I did, you are supposed to do"; right? I would look at his life. He had a goal, a purpose and nothing stopped him. He had liberty. He did what he wanted to do, when he wanted to do it. Sure, I wanted to be that kind of a person, have that kind of liberty; but I would sit back and say to myself, "I can't do that... I can't be that... he was special." I would sit and actually defend my miserable lack of progress. I would justify my limitations and lowly position in life. I could excuse the bad grades, the lack of money and my inability to communicate. My friends at school and work were right there helping me by doing the same thing.

Are you not justifying something now? Are you not saying, "I can't because..."? Are you not doing what I did as a youth? I would like to challenge you to stop justifying. The following exercise may be helpful in identifying common justifications.

JUSTIFICATIONS

Here is a list of all the justifications you ever will need. Circle the ones you use most, and then cross them out of your life forever!

IF I just didn't have a family...
IF I had enough money...
IF only I had a college degree...
IF I just felt better...
IF only I had had the opportunity...
IF it weren't for other people...
IF I had the type of job I really wanted...
IF I were young again...
IF I were older and knew more...
IF I just had some special talent...
IF fate doesn't interfere...
IF the economic condition were better...
IF I could just find the right man/woman...
IF I were not in debt...
IF I had a better childhood...
IF I had a business of my own...
IF I were the boss...
IF I were lucky...
IF my family just understood me...
IF other people would just listen...
IF I were smarter...
IF I lived some place else...
IF I had been born rich...
IF I didn't have to take care of the kids...
IF I had someone to go with...

IF I knew the right people...

IF I had a little political pull...

IF my nature were different...

IF I were sure of what I was doing...

IF I didn't have to work so hard...

IF someone would give me a break...

IF I had a home of my own...

IF I had the time...

IF I could do it all over again...

IF I could express myself better...

IF I knew what they wanted...

IF I had liberty...

IF I were skinny...

IF I were bigger...

IF I had not inherited the traits of my parents...

IF I lived in a better neighborhood...

IF I HAD THE COURAGE TO SEE MYSELF AS I REALLY AM...

    IF...

        IF...

            IF...

The I AM concept is the way to stop justifying.

"For as a man thinketh in his heart so is he." (Prov. 23:7)

What does that mean "thinketh in his heart"? My heart does not think. My subconscious is the part with most of the programs and processes. And that is exactly what it means, "As I believe in my subconscious, so am I." Isn't that beautiful? That one simple statement can tell us why we are as we are. No justifications or complex theology, just a simple statement that everyone can understand. "OK," you say. "I buy that. As I am in my subconcious,

I am." Now, what if I do not like what I am? What if I
am not reaching my full potential? What if I am not experiencing
more of me? The solution is now obvious. If you do not like the
way you are thinking, the way you are in your subconscious, then
change your thinking.

The problem is most people do not know how. It's easy.
Just think about the problem (i.e., direct your *attention*) and
then see the solution repeatedly as you want it to be (i.e., *give
the orders*) through the screen of the mind and affirmations.
Repeated actions become a habit in the subconscious. The
subconscious does not care about right or wrong, good or bad. It
just takes what it gets most often and turns that into a habit pattern,
which ultimately becomes the reality. So if you give the
subconscious pictures and thoughts of what you want to be
often enough, these will become the patterns in the subconscious
level of your personal I AM's.

Every great thinker and positive leader has confirmed this
concept, including Jesus, Buddha, Gandhi, Lao-tse, Mohammed.
Why? Because this is a basic law, a fundamental Truth. And one
of the things we need to realize is that no one lives outside the
law. Ignorance is no excuse. If someone steps off a cliff, the Law
of Gravity doesn't care if it's the noblest person on earth, they're
going down! Either you are liberated by the knowledge of the law,
or you are placed in bondage by ignorance of the law. The law
either sets limits for you, or removes them. Thus, my ignorance
of the law placed me as a youth in bondage to poverty, to low
grades and to feelings of "less than." Now that I have knowledge
of the law, it provides me with the liberty of wealth, intelligence
and self-confidence.

The mind is like a very fertile field. Try a little imagining right now. See in your mind the most fertile field you can create, the soil is dark, moist and rich. Know with assurance that whatever seeds you plant will grow. Most of us do not understand that sowing the seeds once is not enough. As farmers, we must stand there and be a sentinel. We must chop out the weeds; because the weeds, the negativity in life, will destroy or limit the crop. The negativity is there and if we do not stand guard, it will grow as well. Maturity is becoming aware of the responsibility of our minds.

Being mature is more than a physical thing. Dogs, cats and the body mature physically, but human beings mature mentally too. They do this by accepting the responsibility for their thinking. This is the real meaning of maturity. As I began to come out of the ignorance of my youth and understand this concept, I began to work with it for about fifteen minutes each day. My results were very small. The return was tiny. I had a very large garden, as each of us does, and I was working in it only fifteen minutes a day.

The garden of the subconscious needs enough care so that it is balanced. I needed to work on it every minute of every day. The results for me from doing this have been very sweet indeed.

The I AM concept is the foundation of all the concepts. It is the bottom rung on the ladder. You cannot get to the second rung without some understanding of the I AM concept. How do you know whether or not you know this concept? It is simple. The only way to judge is by results. Though often harsh, they are always fair. How do we know we understand the concepts? *By results in life.* By the successes, or lack of them, in our experiences. There is no other valid way. Take a moment now and list your successes. Write down those things that are going right in your life at this moment. How well have you understood the I AM concept in the past?

Mahatma Gandhi spoke of the I AM concept when he said, *"Man is at the center of a circle with an unlimited circumference."* What are your limitations? You can be sure you have them, as long as you have health problems, are subject to the ups and downs of the economy, and are victim to circumstances, as long as there are weeds in your garden.

Awareness and the thoughtful, positive practice of the I AM principle can produce incredible results. It takes a bit of daring to commit to really test the validity of this concept, to experiment with your I AM's. In my case, when I honestly went for it, I suddenly had a life that had meaning. I had liberty to do what I wanted to do, to live the way I wanted to live. I felt better than I had ever felt before.

What are your I AM's? What are the thoughts you think about yourself every day? I do not mean what you would like to be or hope to be, but what you are right now, based on results. If you have not already done so, make a list now of your I AM's before you continue. Most people begin their I AM's something like this: "I am a woman, or a man; I am 38; I am a store owner; I am a parent…" If they have had an awareness class or two, it might start more like this: "I am happy some of the time; I am a lover; I am sad sometimes; I am getting tired of doing this…" All the I AM's listed above are alike; they just have different words. They are all limits on your circumference.

Very few people in this world really comprehend the I AM concept. It is neither an intellectual understanding nor a memory recall. It is a digesting process, so the program becomes a part of you. You begin to experience the I AM on a minute-by-minute basis in your life. And when, by results, your life is out of balance, you can immediately bring it back to balance.

To those that understand, the response to the I AM question is simple. It is, *I am a leader*. Notice your internal emotional reaction to those words. *I am a leader* . We are not talking about being president of a corporation, or a nation, or a leader of people. Those are results of leadership. You can be a leader with no one following you. Instead, I am talking about the internal side of leadership, with you as an individual. I am talking about being a *leader of self*. The unique thing about leaders is that leaders have accepted the responsibility for their thinking. They have accepted the responsibility for the results in their lives. And if they do not like the results, they change them. They take the negative and make it positive. *Leaders accept responsibility*. They understand the sowing process. By controlling the conscious mind, they control the casting of seeds into the subconscious mind. By controlling the way they think, they are accepting the responsibility for what they are.

You are your I AM's, the ones you feel in your gut. Listen to them. And the moment you say, "I refuse to listen to my limitations anymore. I refuse to be this or that. I am happier, healthier, more open, more trusting," you start becoming that way. Every day as you repeat these statements, you move in that direction. A month, three months, a year down the pike, you are happier, healthier, more open and more trusting than you were. "If only I could believe and have faith," you say. That's easy. Just keep lying to yourself long enough and you will believe it. Remember, the subconscious takes what it gets. It takes the orders you consciously give it, right or wrong, true or false, and creates. You do not have to be dishonest. You do not have to go around telling the whole world you are rich if you are not at the moment. You only have to tell yourself that. And tell yourself again and again and again, until you believe it and feel it.

Will you accept the responsibility for you? Do you really want to feel better tomorrow? If you do, watch the seeds you cast today. Watch how you think. Feelings are the result of how you think. You can achieve anything that is positive and worthy of you. The super-conscious is the source of the power. The subconscious will do the work for you. Understand all that is positive and worthy of you is available to you. *You are in tune with the infinite.*

Much of this may seem philosophical and rather theoretical. But my personal experience has been very practical. This is what I do:

I think about my subconscious. I visualize it as being a genie; the same type of all-powerful genie that Aladdin had in his magic lamp. I visualize my genie as being a young girl of about nine or ten with beautiful, flowing, brown hair and big, innocent, brown eyes. I call her Jeanie. I see her as the innocence of youth and yet with a depth in her eyes from which comes power. This is, indeed, the subconscious. It is not chained by custom, culture or guilt; it awaits my every command. Jeanie sits and waits until I send her a command.

After I had discovered the existence of my genie, I said to her, "Jeanie, I want to be wealthy." "OK," she said, "I will bring forth wealth in abundance." Then I said, "Jeanie, I want to be happy. I want to have joy." Again, she went off and set about bringing happiness and joy into my life. Then one day I said, "Jeanie, I'm discouraged." "OK," she said, and brought me discouragement. Then I began to understand a little more about that genie and realized that she listened very carefully to me. Later I said, "Jeanie, I know you can do all things. So go and bring me that high mountain over there. I want that mountain." "Sure," she said, and off she went. Now, as she left, it occurred to me that the mountain is awfully big and no one has ever been able to move it. Before I had even finished the thought, Jeanie walked back through the door. "OK, if that's what you say," she said. At that moment I understood the meaning of the I AM concept. I understood the role of the subconscious. You see, Jeanie, my genie, was listening to even my silent thoughts. I did not have to shout commands to her; she knew even my casual thoughts. "No one has ever been able to move it before" was just another order to her. The subtle suggestion, the little damaging command, these gentle influences are heard by the subconscious. You must have faith and trust in your genie to carry out both the little and the big tasks you assign her. So I started with the little things, things that didn't seem to matter that much. Then, gradually, I trusted her with larger and larger projects until I now have total and complete faith in her abilities. I believe in me. I know that I know that I can.

I started with drawing pictures on the screen of my imagination of how I wanted to be. The expression on my face, the way my hair would look, what I would wear, the personality, and the image I would project. Then I asked Jeanie to create this image just as I saw it. I continued to see in detail every aspect of my new image: a happy person, self-confident and successful. I saw myself being of service, being successful and reaping the rewards of that success. At first I could not afford a dozen designer suits, but I could afford one. My first car was not a Lincoln Continental, but every time I stepped inside the car I had, I saw and experienced the feel of a Lincoln Continental. And Jeanie did her work. I saw and felt and lived the man I wanted to become and now I AM he.

"You are greater than you know."

5

The Book of Mastermind

"Support means taking the responsibility to see that all of your abilities are applied toward the accomplishment of the goal."

Thomas D. Willhite

MASTERMIND

*"For where two or three are gathered in my name, there am I
in the midst of them."
(Matt. 18:20)*

SUMMARY: The key to all power lies within the creation of a Mastermind,
for the Mastermind is the power. Bringing together in harmony the conscious,
subconscious and super-conscious results in the creation of the Mastermind
within you. Join in harmony with others, and the power is unconquerable.
The secret of all power lies within this book, the Mastermind.

What is a thought? Think about it for a moment. *What is
a thought?* I am more than a single thought, yet all my
thoughts taken together form my consciousness as I know it now.
I think of something, but how? Many thoughts are produced by
reflecting and creating. Others just "pop" in as though they had a
beingness of their own. So where did they come from? And how
did I get them? Why did I get them and not someone else? Or did
someone else get them too? In all of life there is no more complex
question than, *"What is a thought?"* Solve this mystery, and you
may very well solve the mystery of life.

Today, scientists tell us that everything we see, feel and
touch is energy. This book is energy, our bodies, the clouds, the
stars, even the air we breathe. The atom, once thought to be
the smallest particle of matter, was split and the result was
stupendous energy. So scientists looked inside the particles which
make up the atom and what they found was energy. The atom
is energy confined to a tiny space. Electricity is a form of energy
in motion. A table is energy molded into a form. All matter is
"condensed energy."

I'm convinced that *thought is energy not yet condensed*. The question is how do we condense a thought? Add more energy. And add it in such a way that all of it works and vibrates together. The result is something powerful that has reality, and it is more than just a sum of the energies which have come together. For when they join in harmony, a force exceeding the sum is unleashed.

To illustrate, you might recall seeing films of the Tacoma Narrows Bridge, which was built in 1940 on Puget Sound in Tacoma, Washington. The bridge was literally torn apart by 40 M.P.H. winds. Most bridges, houses and other structures we build can withstand 40 M.P.H. winds without problems. A shingle may fly off, or there may be some minor damage, but the whole thing does not just collapse. So what was it about that particular bridge which produced enough power to tear it to pieces? It was not the wind alone, because the wind did not have that much force. Scientists and engineers immediately started to work on the problem. This is what they found. It was a suspension bridge and was supported from cables, not too different from the Golden Gate Bridge. As the wind began to blow, the cables began to vibrate. Though not intentionally, the design of the bridge caused the cables to vibrate in resonance (harmony). The cables acted like a child's swing: a very small push on the swing results in a large motion. For the Tacoma Narrows Bridge, the wind repeatedly provided that small push. As the wind increased in velocity, a tremendous force built up within the bridge. By the time the wind had reached 40 M.P.H., the bridge could not stand the stresses and literally destroyed itself. The wind was only the agent which caused the vibrations to be in harmony, not the sole cause.

In this illustration the result of the force might appear to be destructive. In reality, energy is neither positive nor negative, it simply is. That same combination of wind and harmonic vibration could be harnessed toward useful purposes. The resolution of the energy crisis may well lie here. It is all in one's point of view.

A similar force can be unleashed when thought energies are brought together in harmony. This force I call the Mastermind. It is the force and power of the super-conscious coming through when thoughts come together in harmony.

The principles of the Mastermind can be stated as follows:

When two or more minds (thoughts) are brought together and blended in perfect harmony, there is created a third mind, or power, which is different from and greater than the parts which came together. This third mind, or Mastermind, can be used by one or all of the individual minds. It will disappear, and all evidence of its former existence will disintegrate, when the harmonious alliance of the minds is broken.

The Mastermind, that awesome force, is available to you now and will always be available to you. It is accessible in two ways: first, with yourself, through the harmonizing of your conscious mind with the subconscious and the super-conscious, and second, through the creation of Mastermind groups by harmonizing the minds of two or more persons. We shall look at how to create the Mastermind both ways, but first let us consider the key: *Harmony.*

Harmony is the key. This cannot be overemphasized. The lack of harmony is usually the cause of failure. Do you have a marriage that has failed or is failing? Are you in a job that is depressing or frustrating? Look for the lack of harmony, within and without, in these situations.

Now look at your successes and see how their harmony was working for you. Notice how, in the successful situations, those close to you worked with you and supported you toward that goal. All the elements, the pieces and the people, worked together as a unit. This is the meaning of harmony: all the pieces or parts working together toward the same goal.

A healthy human body is a perfect example of harmony. All the subsystems: circulation, nerves, digestion, breathing, work together to produce an active, vibrant, beautiful person. Each subsystem does its own part to support the rest of the systems and the overall well-being of the person. One system is not "better than" another. There are no ego problems. If this harmony is broken by overeating (as when the stomach desires to take control) or by nerves (as when the nervous system takes over) or whatever, the body begins to fail. The result: obesity, nervous breakdown, and disease. Notice, the harmony is broken first, then the failure.

You create the Mastermind power when you harmonize the conscious, subconscious and the super-conscious minds.

This is the source of the personal power of all great leaders: Moses, Lincoln, Joan of Arc, Martin Luther King. In each of these people, there was total agreement, harmony, between the conscious and subconscious minds and this agreement was in accord with the super-conscious, the deep universal senses. As a result, the power of the super-conscious was able to perform what seemed to be superhuman feats. They were not superhuman people. They were leaders who understood the law of harmony and used it. That same power is available to you right now.

Pause quietly for a moment, and see if you can touch base with this power. This is an exercise we do to bring into line our levels of consciousness. Start with a universal concept, such as "peace." See it as a seed deep within. Watch it expand upwards, spreading like a fan of light, illuminating the peace of your subconscious, your I AM's, your program relating to peace, your memories of peacefulness. Now the light floods into your consciousness. Your whole body vibrates, radiating peace outward into your home, your city, your country, the earth itself and on to the very limits of the universe and beyond. Realize that as it expands outward, it grows inward, for the universe is one. The furthermost reaches of the universe are within the depths of your being. It is an endless cycle, an endless source of power.

It is.

The key to harmony is agreement at all levels of consciousness toward a goal. Notice that all great leaders have a strong, overwhelming goal, one to which their whole being, all three levels of consciousness, is committed. And within each level, there is consistency, so that the whole is harmonious. Consider the following example:

OUT OF HARMONY:

"I want lots of money." "I want to be rich." "I want a big house."

"I AM not educated and education is necessary to get ahead."

"I AM like my mother/father and they had to struggle."

"Rich people aren't happy."

(Money does not exist for the super-conscious; money is a creation of the conscious mind. Hence, "money" has no meaning in the superconscious.)

IN HARMONY:

"I want to be justly rewarded in proportion to the service I render to mankind."

"I want to be of service."

"I always have all that I need. I AM perfect as I am and as I am becoming."

"I have the abilities to do what I need to do and ample time to accomplish my goals."

"There is infinite supply."

In the "Out of Harmony" example, there appears to be no disagreement on the conscious level. But the subconscious level is a different story. The conscious and the subconscious of this individual are in conflict. Furthermore, the conscious goals do not match up with the super-conscious since the goal is meaningless outside the conscious realm. The experience of the person, who is out of harmony, is probably one of ups-and-downs and confusion. On the other hand, the person who is "In Harmony" has goals which are compatible. The I AMs support the conscious goals and draw from the infinite supply of the super-conscious. Such a person would appear to have an unlimited supply of all things he needs and that would include money. He or she would be a person of strength and power.

The result of harmony between the three levels of consciousness is power. It is the ability to get what you need when you need it; to do what you want to do when you want to do it; to be what you want to be when you want to be it.

The effects of the Mastermind will appear in many ways: sudden inspirations; "lucky" breaks; those amazing coincidences;

things effortlessly falling into place; attracting the right people with the right skills, resulting in the perfect manifestation of the goal in the shortest time. The process may well include hard work, but there will also be a sense of ease and pleasure.

The growth of leaders begins here, with the creation of the Mastermind within.

This book began with a quotation from the Bible, "For where two or three are gathered together in my name, there am I in the midst of them" (Matt. 18:20). This could easily be referring to the Mastermind, the godlike power, which emerges when minds are united in harmony towards a positive goal. The Mastermind results not only from harmony within, but also can result when two or more persons achieve this same harmony between themselves. Again, the key is *harmony* and the result is power.

Unlimited power is available to those men and women who have the wisdom and determination to submerge personalities, egos and personal interests through the blending of their minds in harmony towards a specific purpose. Jesus and his disciples formed just such a Mastermind. So did Marie and Pierre Curie (discoverers of radium). Ford, Edison and Firestone all founded their initial companies with Mastermind teams. In fact, the modern corporation is based on the Mastermind principle. The Mastermind team in corporations is the Board of Directors. The people who make up this team control the direction and ultimate outcome of a corporation.

But not every Board of Directors is a Mastermind team, though they do have the potential to become one. Neither is every group of individuals who come together in cooperation towards a common purpose a Mastermind. The Mastermind will not spring up just because you get a group together and decide to do something. There is a lot hidden in that little word *harmony*. For the harmony of purpose between the individuals must exist at *all* levels of consciousness. There must be not only conscious-level agreement, but also subconscious-level agreement. The superconscious is always in agreement because it is universal, common to all. Thus, each individual is in harmony with themselves and at the same time in harmony with all levels of every other member of the Mastermind team.

The process is easy to describe but often difficult in real life. First, it is necessary to arrive at a conscious agreement. This usually can be done fairly quickly. Then the harder task comes: to achieve a subconscious agreement. This means that every program and I AM must be in harmony and support your I AMs. I cannot hold onto old programs about having to be "the best" and fit in the Mastermind. It will not work. My immediate and personal interests must submerge to the overall purpose of the Mastermind. Is this not the true meaning of teamwork? You will find the Mastermind principle working in the team that could not possibly make it to the Championship finals, but did, or in the family that started a business with all the cards stacked against them and succeeded.

The following is an illustration of the way harmony is established between two individuals in order that the Mastermind can emerge. First, conscious agreement on the goal is established. Next, the two people work to establish the subconscious agreements between themselves, at the same time maintaining harmony within their own conscious/subconscious levels; then, if these agreements are in harmony with the super-conscious, the Mastermind power emerges.

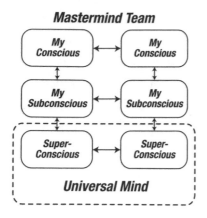

Mastermind Team

Conscious Agreement: We want to establish a PSI Center in this city where the PSI programs can be taught. This will work towards the goal of peace in our lifetime. You will be the City Manager...I will be the Assistant City Manager.

Subconscious Agreement: I am perfect; you are perfect; we are becoming more perfect. I am learning; you are learning; we are learning together. We are equals; each of our jobs is equally important for the achievement of our goals.

Superconscious Agreement: Everything is perfect just as it is, and just as it is becoming.

The results of creating a Mastermind are awesome. It is peace, power and knowing all in one. It is unbounded ideas and limitless energy. It is knowing that you know.

"This is all very good," you say, "but I do not know anyone with whom I can create such a Mastermind team." No? You know yourself, and that is where to begin. Create the Mastermind within your three levels of consciousness. Use your imagination, your workshop and assistants to help. In fact, you can create in your mind your own personal Mastermind team there in your workshop. Whom do you know, or have you heard of, who would be most helpful in achieving your goal? Bring that person into your workshop and build a Mastermind. Is there another person your team needs? Then bring that person in also. Remember, at the subconscious level of mind you have unlimited resources. You can include whomever you wish. As you establish a Mastermind within your three levels of consciousness and bring your own being into harmony, you will naturally attract others of like interests and desires. With these people you can begin to establish your external Mastermind. How many should be included in a Mastermind? As many as you want. Jesus brought twelve together to form a

Mastermind of thirteen. Successful marriages have a Mastermind of two at their core.

Not all minds can be harmonized together and blended into a Mastermind. Not all people are alike in thinking, nor would we want them to be. You will be able to form a Mastermind with one person but not another. This is not a right/wrong situation. It is simply what it is. One of the major responsibilities of a leader is to position people in such a way that Mastermind teams can be formed. They are placed at strategic points in the organization and in such combinations so that their individual minds will blend in harmony with each other and with the leader's purpose. The ability to organize is one of the primary characteristics of a leader, who must also know and understand the Mastermind principle and apply it personally first. A leader is first a leader of self and only then, a leader of others.

Many of the most effective Mastermind alliances result from the blending of the minds of domestic partners. I suspect the reason is that where love and intimacy are present, minds will more readily harmonize. With fewer areas of conflict at the subconscious level, agreements come easier. They can support one another with genuine belief in their individual goals and endeavors. It is extremely powerful to know the person who is closest is on your side no matter what. The messages are these: "I believe in you." "I know you can do it." "If you don't feel good in this job, this transaction, this pursuit, then let's find one that's right." "What can I do to help?" "I think you're perfect just as you are."

On the other hand, those same people constantly disagreeing with each other at the conscious and subconscious levels will result in sure defeat. Because of ego, the need to be "right," or a fear of losing control, people too often get together and start suppressing each other. Throwing cold water on the other's dreams, cutting remarks, selfishness, undermining, domineering, passive aggression, vanity, are some of the poisons guaranteed to kill a relationship.

Life was meant to be a success for each partner. The Mastermind grows in an environment of love and trust, which adds to the power. It would be ideal if one could find the perfect mate, who is already in total harmony with your thinking and your goals at both the conscious and subconscious levels. This probably will not happen. Most couples, when they set up a permanent relationship, do not know their own goals, let alone know if their partner is in harmony with them. Wisdom would say to look before you leap, but most people just leap.

Perhaps you are married, or living with someone, or simply involved, and your goals are not in total harmony at the present time. Does that mean you cannot have a Mastermind? The answer is "no" and "yes." "No," you do not have a Mastermind at the present time, and "yes" you probably can create one if you are willing to put effort into it. A Mastermind is not "instant coffee." You cannot mix two people together and get instant Mastermind, even if they are in love. Many times in a relationship, each partner expects the other to have their same goals. Not so. Establishing a Mastermind is a *communication process*. It is something you must consciously decide to do. The communication must take place at both the conscious (goal) level and the subconscious (feelings, programs) level. With an awareness of where conflicts lie, the couple can work toward harmony. Each partner will have to make adjustments.

If you are still of the opinion that your partner needs to do all the changing, I suggest you re-read this book from the beginning.

In a Mastermind, personal interests and goals are subordinate to the Mastermind group's goal. A dictatorship is where the leader's personal interests and goals dominate.

Once the Mastermind has been built, it will require constant attention. However, do not confuse "attention" with work or effort. A pilot must constantly watch his instruments and verify his position. This does not mean the pilot is changing course every five minutes or even adjusting the controls. It does mean that the pilot is always aware of the location of the aircraft and where it is going. Likewise in the Mastermind, the leader will check the team to see where they are and where they are going. Again, it is a communication process, essential for the maintenance of all relationships and all Masterminds.

A family can form a powerful Mastermind team. History supplies numerous illustrations of such Mastermind groups. In the Middle Ages, the Medici family claimed tremendous political and economic power in Italy. In more recent times, we see a concentration of power in such well-known families as the Roosevelts, the Kennedys and the Rockefellers. The leaders within each of these families are well-known. Look more closely, and you will find other, equally strong family members. The significant role Rose Kennedy played within her family, or Eleanor Roosevelt within hers, cannot be denied.

Each family who wishes to form a harmonious team will come to its own way of adjusting to each other's goals. The Mastermind does not require a set pattern, but instead results from harmony and agreement among the members. Thus, in one family there may be a single financial provider and the other manages the domestic chores. In another, the financial responsibilities, as well as household responsibilities, may be shared. There is no right or wrong here. The individuals involved must achieve the harmony within the context of their own goals. The goals of the individuals need not be the same, but they must be in harmony, that is, mutually supported by the others involved.

Sometimes a husband or wife will choose to play the role of critic. A critic is essentially an outside evaluator, someone who is not on the team. You cannot be both on the team and off at the same time. It simply will not work. If you choose to be a part of a Mastermind team, then be a part of it, through total support. Giving support also means doing your share, not one member being a competitive business partner or any other opposing role. A team where one person dominates and makes all the decisions is not a team.

Support means taking the responsibility to see that all your abilities are applied toward the accomplishment of the goal.

If you are part of a Mastermind and find you can no longer support it, then disassociate yourself from the team. By so doing, you allow the Mastermind to continue. If you remain, your discontent will create the negative force that causes the Mastermind power to fail. You will become the Judas of your Mastermind group. Once you are outside the Mastermind, you can pursue your own goals. The results are positive all around. You win by staying in alignment with your own conscious and subconscious directions. The others win by being given the same opportunity. How often companies, both small and large, falter and even fail because one person was not strong enough to step away from the organization they could no longer support. If you work for a company, for goodness sake support that company. Support its goals and the decisions of its officers. And if you cannot, then quit. Do not be the one who backbites, criticizes, causes turmoil and collapse from within. Disassociate yourself from the company. *Then* say what you will, as loud as you please. Such a person is a leader of self.

Built on harmony, the Mastermind results in a power or force that is far greater than the sum of the parts. Each person in the Mastermind is vested with this power. Each person will experience greater energy, more vivid imagination, increased awareness ness, more ideas, a drawing in of other minds of like character, a sense of control and purpose. The Mastermind team becomes like a magnet, attracting all that they need from the universe around them. The better the alignment of the individuals, the more powerful the magnet. Yet, when the harmony is broken, the power fails. The failure is often sudden and complete. If you are familiar with an electromagnet, it is the same effect as turning off the switch. The power is gone. Everything stops. Among groups, the Mastermind fails when one or more persons become out of harmony. By this I mean that their goals are no longer the group's goals. Personal interests have taken precedence.

If a Mastermind has failed, it is *not* possible to just eliminate the problem person and keep going. The power is gone. What is left of the group must form anew. They must establish again the agreement between their conscious and subconscious levels under the current circumstances. Thus, a new Mastermind team is formed, one which may have grown out of, but is totally different from, the former. Christianity is the result of such a re-forming. When one of the disciples, Judas Iscariot, broke the faith, he broke the Mastermind. The immediate result was total disintegration. During the night of betrayal, the disciples scattered, lost their power, lost faith; and confusion reigned. Since Jesus himself did not lose faith, he personally did not lose power. His internal Mastermind power remained intact. After the death of Jesus, the disciples that remained re-formed the Mastermind. Out of this new Mastermind came Christianity as we know it today.

There are many important insights into building Masterminds in this example, far beyond the religious significance. For example, once the Mastermind is established, it is not essential for the people to be physically together, although it is easier. In later years the disciples scattered, yet the power went with them. It is not necessary for there to be a legal bond among the group. The bond of harmony is far stronger. As you think upon this powerful Mastermind, perhaps the most powerful in our recorded history, you will find even more insights. I leave these for you to discover, using the Mastermind formed with your own conscious, subconscious and super-conscious levels.

6

THE BOOK OF WEALTH

"Man is paid in direct proportion to the service he renders mankind"

Thomas D. Willhite

WEALTH

"Our most valuable possessions are those which can be shared without lessening: those which, when shared, multiply. Our least valuable possessions are those which, when divided, are diminished."
~ William H. Danforth

SUMMARY: The laws of wealth are simple. There are but two: first, find a need and fill it, and second, give what you would desire. The application of these rules or laws is all that stands between you and wealth. Riches, materially and spiritually, await those who hear the message of this book with their inner ear.

Do you desire wealth? Be honest with yourself. Would you like to have enough money to do what you want to do? I desire wealth. Every thinking person alive desires it, including those who already have it. There are many who would try to deny this fact. "Only the crooked, or genius," they say, "can gain wealth." Others claim, "The poor are more spiritual." "We have no desire for material goods, so we don't need wealth," cry many others. These statements are not truths; they are justifications for the lack of progress and control in people's lives. Those who condemn wealth are quite often the ones who don't have it now and see no way of gaining it. They take the fear of failure and translate it into the love of poverty. If I believe I'm protecting myself from failure by having no goals, I do not have to face the awful realization that there is something about me which needs re-thinking. The truth is, when I have no goals, I can't succeed. If I do not admit a desire for wealth, I will never obtain it.

"Poverty is no disgrace to a man, but it is confoundedly inconvenient."
~ Sidney Smith

"I've been rich and I've been poor. Rich is better."

- Al Capp

There is absolutely nothing wrong with being prosperous. It is a natural desire to have the things you need and want and know they'll be there tomorrow. Affluence is an obvious help in achieving liberty. In all forms—cash, gold, jewels, stocks, bonds, property, contracts, royalties—wealth is only a commodity of exchange. It is what we give to get what we want. The value lies in its exchangeability, not in the material substance. Gold does not make a tasty dish, nor do diamonds provide much shelter over your head. It is only in the exchange for food or housing that this "wealth" has meaning.

As a child, I was told, "Money is the root of all evil." As an adult, I understand the meaning of this statement. When we worship money, hoard it, make it our god, it is evil, that is, destructive to self. Actually, the Biblical admonition is, "The *love* of money is the root of all evil." As a means of exchange, money is neither good nor bad. It is merely a tool.

Wealth is meant to be used. What we do not use, we lose. This is the Law of Use. The parable of the talents and the three servants is a good illustration. The first two servants took the talents given by the master and put them to use, but the third servant buried his in the ground. A year later the master returned. The first two servants were allowed to keep their talents, which, by this time, had multiplied many folds. But all was taken from the third servant who had let his talents lie idle. He was placed in bondage.

There are only two rules about material wealth and they are very simple. One concerns its creation; the other is how to become a receiver. You can grow to be very, very wealthy through the use of these two rules. First, they must be understood. Then they may be translated and applied to your specific situation. The results will be awesome, *but don't take my word for it.* Try it for yourself. Experiment and experience. Then, use the results you get in your own life - not my results, nor your neighbors' - to decide if these rules are to become a permanent part of your living pattern.

To create wealth, all you have to do is *find a need and fill it.* The greater the need, the more people will be happy to pay. So if you are having problems in your business and your income is not as high as you would like, look at the needs of the people with whom you do business. Perhaps they do not need your product or service. Find a greater need and fill that need. Your income will increase automatically because the greater the need, the more people will pay for it.

The rule applies in a far broader spectrum than just obtaining material wealth. It applies to the winning of friends and gaining promotions. In the larger sense, it translates this way: *people have everything you will ever want, and they will gladly give it to you, provided you help them get what they want.* Find a need and fill it. Be of service.

The above is only an application of a basic law, which is far more inclusive. It applies to all of living, all of experiencing. In reality, wealth is Life. Your wealth is the sum total of all you have and all you experience. Material wealth refers to all the earthly goods you have. The laws of material wealth are the basic laws of life applied in the direction of material things. The basic law is this: *Man is paid in direct proportion to the service he renders mankind.*

The greater the service, the more one is paid. If you want to gauge your service, look at your income and your experiences. Material wealth is a measuring stick for service. Wealth is the result of rendering service. I do not work for wealth. Working for wealth is the "love of money." If all you get at the end of the week is a paycheck, then you are highly cheated - by yourself. If you desire to increase your wealth, increase your service to mankind.

Wise people do not give service for free. They always charge a fair price, realizing that nothing is free. "*There ain't no free lunch.*" The service will be paid for either monetarily or otherwise. The PSI classes are not given for free. How many people would accept the PSI concept and believe in it if it were free? Very, very few. They would not know how to attach a value to PSI. So, in ignorance, they would assume it was worth nothing. They would lose the opportunity to create liberty, peace and love in their lives. The price is paid one way or another. So whatever it is that you do making pottery, a garden business, teaching, running a service station, sewing, engineering, counseling feel confident in charging a fair price. A fair price is one which is equal to the service rendered. Competition has nothing to do with a "fair price."

To increase your wealth, increase your service. All you have to do is apply this simple law to your business or profession. An example from the everyday competitive world in which we live might begin with an intersection, one of those busy ones where two main streets cross. Imagine there are four gas stations, one on each corner. One might think there would be heavy competition there. Not necessarily. Actually, there is no such thing as competition *except for those people who choose to place themselves in competition.* If you see the situation as competitive, then you will, indeed, be in competition with the other filling stations. You are setting yourself up to lose. Competition is a win-lose situation. Either I win and the rest of you lose, or I lose and one of you wins. It happens every day. Filling station #1 lowers its price to try to get ahead of the competition. Stations #2 and #4 follow suit, while station #3 goes even a cent lower. Stations #2 and #4 are now hurting, so the next day they lower their price two cents. To maintain themselves, the stations must cut service and wages.

By trying to be competitive, these stations would price themselves right out of business. Not even the customer would win, because if they all fail, then the motorist has to find somewhere where else to get gas. Or, if only one gas station remains, then the price might go up. There are not very many winners in competitive situations.

But suppose station #2 gets tired of the rat race. He decides to come to a PSI class and finds out there is another way: I win; you win. He is no longer interested in being in competition with the others. He sets a fair price on his gas. Quite often, it will be two to three cents per gallon higher than the surrounding places. It is a fair price because he gives you the very best service in town and he pays the highest wages to his attendants. Despite "selfserve," when you drive into his service station, you will have an attendant who will help fill the tank, check under the hood, and like a friendly spirit of the past, actually clean your windows. Why does the station do all this? To sell you a new fan belt or air filter? No, their object is to honestly provide you with the best service possible. So when you have a car problem, where would you go? Which station will get your business? I know which one would get mine.

The above illustration is not hypothetical; it is real. When my wife and I moved to Milwaukee, I looked for just such a station. It took me a whole month before I finally found one. I checked over the entire operation. Everything was spotless, even the lube room. Cars were backed up waiting to be worked on. There were no cut-rate deals at that station; no bargain rates. Gas was two cents higher than the station across the street. "This is the man I want," I thought. I walked in and said to the manager, "I have a special problem. I travel three or four weeks out of the month. I have a wife and children. They need a car that is dependable, one that starts even in a blizzard and doesn't break down on the road. The car will need maintenance, and I need you to decide what is to be done. Don't call my wife because she's not a car person. She'll bring the car in whenever you say." The man had integrity. He kept records on the car, called it in when necessary and took good care of it. All I ever got from him were bills, which I was happy to pay. He ran his business to serve. I wanted him to be paid well because I appreciated his concern, especially in that winter weather. *People are paid in direct proportion to the service they render mankind.*

Apply this idea of service to your business, whatever that may be. The above station owner was too busy to worry about the competition. All he cared about was what was right and having a relationship that was "win-win" with his customers. Create that attitude in your business, and you will not have to look for customers, they will come to you. There are many services you can give and enjoy doing. But the price that people will pay is in proportion to the need. So the "need" is where you must go to analyze the service. Based on the need, a fair price is placed on the service. To increase your income, increase your service; fill a greater need.

"All right," you say, "I understand that, but I don't own my own company and I don't have customers. I work for a company and am only one small part of what we do. I don't set policies. I follow them. How am I supposed to increase service?" The service an employee renders is to his employer. Therefore, increase your service to your employer. In other words, *cultivate the habit of doing more than you are paid for* and do it cheerfully. What if every night you started studying your profession so you would know more? What if you volunteered for those tasks, which others shirk, either because they are difficult, or because there is no pay for doing them? What would happen if you were the most knowledgeable, skilled and up-to-date person in your field? Then, what if you started going to work ten or fifteen minutes early each day to get yourself organized? Instead of entering right on the dot and sitting around with a cup of coffee, you are ready and working five minutes before check-in time. What if you stopped clock-watching and forgot about breaks because you were totally into a project, producing results for your company? What if you brown-bagged a couple of lunches each week, or worked right through the lunch hour? What if you stayed an extra fifteen minutes at the end of the day to wrap things up and get organized for tomorrow? What if you were always positive with the other employees, instead of buying their negativty? When you walk into the office feeling great and someone "growls" at you, do you get angry, defensive, or depressed? If so, you bought into their negativity. So what if you stopped buying negativity and started selling a positive attitude? I can guarantee you one of two things will happen. Either you will get promoted to the top because you have displayed leadership abilities, or you'll get fired, because you rattled the troops. You will be so unusual that you will stick out like a sore thumb. It is not normal to be excited about your job. It is not normal to be excited about your employer making a profit. However, these feelings are natural when you understand the laws of wealth and when you know your reward is in direct proportion to the service you render. This is the start on the road to wealth.

In all my years of work, I have had few people come to me and say, "Mr. Willhite, I see that you have such and such a problem. This is what I can do to help solve it for you." Most people come to me and say, "I want to work for you. How much do I get paid and what are the fringe benefits? Tell me what to do." I do not need this latter type of employee. They are the takers. They obsess about whether the person at the next desk is getting paid more and doing less. They rarely think about getting the job done, or what's good for the company. Such people do not last very long in my business and they certainly do not move up in the company.

On the road to wealth and success there is one very large stumbling block. It is a mountain that stands between most people and their ability to give service to their employer, or customers. It is the feeling that you are being cheated if you do not immediately receive money for all the services you render. Most people say, "I'll try this for a day or two, or even a month and see what happens." Often nothing happens... that they can see. They do not instantly get the big raise and their volume of business has not doubled overnight. "Well, I guess this doesn't work for me," they say and give up. They have run smack into that mountain. How long have you been running programs of only doing that for which you are paid? How long have you been thinking of wealth as just your paycheck? I do not mean to imply that it cannot happen instantly. It can, but it may not. Similarly, your payment may come in your paycheck, or it may come some other way: a new job offer, a promotion, a company car, fringe benefits. Find a need and fill it. *Serve.*

The law is universal. *You will be paid directly in proportion to the service you render to mankind.* To know that you know this law, you must experience it. I suggest the following experiment: each day for the next two months, render a service to at least one person for which you neither expect nor accept money. Give this service only for the benefit of serving and do it willingly. It does not matter what the service is, nor for whom it is performed. The results will be amazing.

So far I have only mentioned creating wealth. There is another way to obtain wealth: through receiving it. This is a method taught and practiced by most major religions. It is known as *tithing*. Historically, the word "tithe" meant one tenth. I like to call it "seed money." Seed money refers to setting aside ten percent (a tithe) or more of your income and using this money to spread positive action and values. Generally, this is done by supporting an institution such as a church, or other nonprofit organizations engaged in such work.

If you think about the meaning of seed money, you will know where it must be given. The purpose is to acknowledge the true source of supply. Giving to your family, friends or neighbors, though these are all good acts, does not count as seed money. Giving to scientific research or community projects comes closer. Anyone with a high awareness knows the world needs spiritual understanding and knowledge. When every person has awareness of such knowledge and uses it creatively, then the political and social problems which we now experience will resolve themselves automatically.

Understanding the basis for seed money makes you a trustee for mankind. Under your control is what you call "your" wealth. Use that gift wisely, for the benefit of all mankind, and even more will come under your control *for the use of all mankind*. The end towards which seed money is directed is the spreading of Truth. With all your awareness and knowledge, select that organization or activity, which best achieves this goal. That is where to give your seed money.

I further suggest you give it anonymously, for in so doing you truly are giving to give. The applause for your gifts, especially if they are large ones, robs you of the value of seed money. Applause distracts from the purpose. Down the line, you may discover you are giving to get applause and have lost the true value of giving. There is absolutely no obligation for anyone to give seed money until they reach a state of consciousness where they want to do so. As you go along the path of awareness, there will come a time when this will be a natural expression of your growth. If you give out of a sense of duty, fear, or superstition, then only more fear will come to you. It is better not to give than to give with the wrong attitude. Frequently I hear, "I really want to give, and will, just as soon as things look up, or the kids get older, or..." If you find yourself using such excuses, you have missed the whole point. The greater the present need, the greater the need for giving seed money and the greater the need to acknowledge the true source of supply. Difficulties are an indication of an incorrect mental attitude. They will disappear only when the mental attitude changes. Seed money, given with spiritual understanding, indicates such a change.

How much to give? Traditionally, according to Hebrew law, it is ten percent. The Levitical law required the Hebrews to render unto the service of God one-tenth portion of all the produce of the earth and herds. Throughout the Old Testament continual reference is made to the need and benefits of tithing. If you are concerned about whether to give ten percent of your gross pay or ten percent of your take-home pay, or ten percent of what is left over after expenses, then I suggest you are perhaps not ready to give anything.

The means of receiving wealth through the practice of giving seed money is also founded upon a basic law: *you receive back that which you give*; as you sow, so shall you reap; like attracts like; what you are to the universe, the universe will be to you. No man or woman escapes these laws. You will both rise and prosper though them, or you will be in bondage under them.

If a person has a million dollars locked in a vault and never touched, is he wealthy? If you fear losing your wealth when you give substantial material gifts, are you free? In both cases, I believe you are in bondage to your wealth. Only through giving can you demonstrate strength. Giving is an acknowledgement that whence this came there is more. In fact, there is an infinite supply. If I give all away, I will create more. I do not suggest that you instantly go out and give everything you own away. That would be foolish. First, demonstrate your understanding of the laws of creating and receiving wealth. You will know when you truly understand by the results in your life, specifically, by the amount of wealth you control.

Tithing, sharing and giving are all ways of expressing gratitude. To express gratitude through words alone is hollow. Action is needed. How do you say "Thank you" for sunshine or health, for clear days or gentle rains, for happiness, joy or love? You say it by sharing what you have. You say it by making the world a better place in which to live. You say it by recognizing the true source of all supply. The world is not yours; it is not mine; it is ours. Gratitude is the awareness and thankfulness for all things received.

Money handling is a key in developing wealth and wealth consciousness. This is not difficult; it just requires a system. Many leaders use the following:

~10% of all monies received are given to a humanitarian organization for the betterment of mankind (seed money).

~10% of what is received goes into a savings account, or is invested to increase total net worth.

~25% of what is received goes to pay off debts or loans.

~Taxes are taken out of the remainder.

What is left is for use on food, entertainment, clothes, etc. The first area, seed money, has already been discussed. The second ond ten percent represents what you pay yourself. After working all week, the least you deserve is ten percent. This money goes into a savings account and you do not touch it. If you want to invest your savings, go to a money specialist. When you have car trouble, you go to an auto mechanic. When you do not feel well, you go to a doctor. So when you want to invest your savings, see a money specialist. Make sure it is someone who has integrity and, by results in their own life, can demonstrate they know how to make money grow. The next twenty-five percent goes toward the payment of car loans, house payments and any other notes or debts you may have. If your current payments on debts exceed 25% of your income, you have a problem, one which you seriously need to think about solving. If you are currently paying less than 25% to clear debts, then you might wish to increase your savings or seed money, or just enjoy it. Out of the remaining 55%, next comes taxes, federal, state, local and any others you might owe. Finally, what is left for normal living expenses and for "freedom money" – money for you to do what you want to do.

Follow this simple plan and you will find that you are building wealth every single month. The following table shows how a hypothetical person making $3,000 per month would use the system. The space on the right is for you to add your own figures appropriate for your income level and your debts and taxes.

GROSS EARNINGS	$3,000/month	_____
SEED MONEY	$300/month	_____
SAVINGS	$300/month	_____
DEBTS	$750/month	_____
TAXES	$600/month	_____
LIVING EX. & FREEDOM MONEY	$1050/month	_____

One reaction I always get from those with low salaries or on a tight budget to the above numbers is a cry of protest. "$1050.00 is supposed to pay rent, food *and* give me some freedom money? You must be kidding!" Most renters, however, do not have large debt payments - perhaps a car, but usually not a house payment. Combining these two categories would give a total of $1800.00 for debts, living expenses and freedom money. However, I should point out to renters that, in reality, they are paying off someone else's debt. Those of you who are currently renting might find it wise to consult a money specialist about the other choices available to you: home ownership, condominiums, lease options and investment property. Not only do these options often provide large tax savings, they also keep your money working for you.

Where is your money going? Write down all the expenses you had last month in the categories given above: seed money, savings, debts, taxes, living expenses. How does the way you *actually* spend money compare with the plan used by myself and by many other leaders? Is there a lot of money for which you cannot account, which just got spent somehow? Do you give one category preference over all others?

Saving money is simply a matter of habit. Once established in your life pattern, it will become so automatic you will scarcely be aware of it. People who are always short of funds have a habit of spending money. Have you ever noticed that no matter how much money they earn, there is never enough? And usually these people cannot even explain how the money was spent. Money just seems to disappear for them. They usually have a poverty consciousness, which will keep them in the poorhouse until such time that their thinking changes. It is just the reverse for people with the savings habit. They are always able to save something, no matter how little they may earn. What is more important is the savings habit creates in your consciousness an awareness that you are never poor and that your income is constantly rising. Few people realize the rate at which systematic savings build. A mere $5.00 a day builds to $1,825 by the end of the year. In ten years it's $18,250.00, not counting interest, or profit on investments, which could easily double it. Startling when you consider how easy it is to blow $5.00 a day and not even remember how.

If you fix in your mind the idea that your earning ability is limited, then indeed it is. You will never earn more than that selfset limit. The subconscious will create and maintain the limits you set. With a savings habit, income is constantly increasing. Likewise, net worth is on an uphill path. The message to the subconscious is, "I am more prosperous. I have more wealth." Gradually, selfconfidence, enthusiasm and the feeling of wealth will replace any negative conditioning. This new attitude we call prosperity consciousness. Soon you will begin to anticipate higher levels of prosperity for yourself. You will expect to earn more and have more, and you will. Prosperity consciousness does not come with a set level of income; rather it is the result of an attitude about the availability of wealth for you.

Saving money, creating wealth and giving seed money all deal with wealth in a material sense. In reality, however, wealth is in the mind. True wealth is knowledge. What you know, what you can do and what you can create is the real wealth in your life. This is the basis from which all your material wealth springs. An old proverb says, "Give a man a fish, and you feed him for a day. Teach a man to fish, and you feed him for a lifetime." So it is with wealth. Give a person money, and you give the gift of dependency. Give a person the knowledge of how to gain wealth, and you give the gift of independence and liberty. What greater gift could there be?

You give but little when you give of your possessions. It is when you give of yourself that you truly give. For what are your possessions but things you keep guard for fear you may need them tomorrow?"
~ Kahlil Gibran

7

The Book of Wisdom

"Wisdom is hindsight...
20/20 vision...
in forward motion."

Thomas D. Willhite

WISDOM

"Ask any wise man what he desires most and he will more than
likely say, 'More wisdom.'"
~ Napoleon Hill

SUMMARY: Wisdom is knowing and doing today what feels good tomorrow. Unfortunately, most people find it easier to be wise for others than for themselves. Wisdom is simple, not complex; it is available to all because it comes through the super-conscious. In this book, we will look at the meaning of "being wise" and how to develop that attribute.

Enlightenment is knowing that *everything is perfect just as it is right now*. When this is comprehended, one is enabled to live in total serenity. Everything is perfect. This may seem like a fallacy. "How," you might say, "can everything be perfect when I have this toothache, or cancer, or I have no money, or I'm lonely?" Where is the perfection in war and hate?

Let me give you an example to illustrate the meaning of perfection. Before the 19th century, the quill was the principal writing instrument. It was perfect. Next came the steel-pointed pen, then fountain pen. They were perfect. Then the ballpoint pen appeared. Again, perfect. Now in laboratories scientists are developing the laser beam pen, which can write on paper without burning it, or on metal. It, too, is perfect. There is a big difference between the quill and the laser pen, yet each is perfect, because each was created in someone's mind, then became a physical reality. Of course, there has been tremendous improvement from quill to laser. Seeing different end products, we might be tempted to say the quill is not perfect because it can be improved upon. Enlightenment is knowing that perfection lies in the creative process and therefore the quill is perfect. Similarly, war, disease, hate, as well as love, cooperation and health, are perfect creations. Everything is perfect just as it is right now.

Wisdom is knowing how to change something to make it better. It comes by saying, "Let's do those things that are creative and productive for tomorrow." The Eastern teachings say, "If it feels good, do it." Most people misinterpret this statement. Instead of hearing the Truth in the statement, they hear, "If it feels good physically, I can do it," or "If it feels good intellectually, I can do it," or "If it feels good today, I can do it." Thus, many people do things today and regret them tomorrow. Abuse of alcohol and drugs are examples of today pleasures that become tomorrow regrets. Revenge, hate, jealousy, envy are other examples. People use the phrase "it feels good" as a license to do anything, whether such action leads to enlightenment or enslavement. It would be better to say, "*If it feels good tomorrow, do it.*" That means the criterion for deciding to do or not do a given thing is never the immediate pain or pleasure produced, but rather the future benefits produced for yourself and mankind.

Some people argue that "doing today what feels good tomorrow" is like living in the future. I say not. A wise person understands that time is our most precious commodity. If you must constantly overcome regrets, you are wasting time. We are given only so much time in this life to accomplish the work we have to do. The important time is *now*. What we were or did before this birth is not relevant, neither is what happens after this lifetime. Whatever the hereafter may be, I am convinced our present life and accomplishments here will play a part. Otherwise, there would be no point in living, no point in facing the problems, the struggles and the pain. If the hereafter is so beautiful, then why not just lie down and die now? Why even go through this period of time as a human being? Wisdom is knowing there is a purpose for being alive. We have a destiny. I do not mean being an executive, a rodeo queen, a salesperson, or any particular occupation. I mean becoming all that we can become, enlightened persons, who are of service to mankind. And by doing so, we can move onward to a higher level of being. This is not implying some form of reincarnation. I'm not even sure it exists. It doesn't really matter, unless one is using it as a handy excuse to explain why he is the way he is and therefore avoiding the responsibility for his own life.

Actually, we are the sum total of our thoughts. We are responsible for ourselves. If you do not like the way you feel, change the way you think. Wisdom is knowing how to change to make your life more fulfilling within the span of your given time.

There is nothing mysterious or difficult about changing. But in our lack of understanding, we often create thinking patterns that are full of fear, defense and self-destruction. In this mental state, what needs to be changed seems beyond our comprehension. This is false reasoning. When something appears complex or hard to accomplish, it often may be simplified by envisioning a clear mental picture of what needs to be done. To prove this to yourself, do the "SIMPLE-COMPLEX" exercise on the opposite page.

When you have finished marking each activity on the scale of simple to complex, go back and review it. Are not the "simple" things those things you have done and know how to do, while the "complex" things are those which are "unknown" to you, or things where you are unsure of yourself? Let me give you another

SIMPLE VS COMPLEX

Mark each activity according to how simple or complex you perceive that activity to be by placing an "X" on the scale.

For me, this activity would be:
Simple (Easy)　　Complex (Hard)

Figuring out how much 10 lbs of potatoes would cost	S .C
Solving a mathematical formula for an unknown	S .C
Writing a letter about what you are doing today	S .C
Writing a novel of about 500 pages in length	S .C
Driving a car with automatic transmission	S .C
Driving a car with stick shift	S .C
Flying a single engine airplane	S .C
Walking, driving or hiking	S .C
Water skiing or snow skiing	S .C
Preparing a meal for my family	S .C
Preparing a french pastry for dessert	S .C
Putting together a jigsaw puzzle	S .C
Assembling a do-it-yourself radio/television kit	S .C
Doodling	S .C
Doing an oil portrait	S .C

Look back over the items you have marked as "complex." Are these not areas where you do not know how to do something... or perhaps an area you have never tried? Unknown! Now look at the things you have done often. Things you know how to do? *ALL THINGS ARE AS SIMPLE OR COMPLEX AS WE PERCEIVE THEM TO BE.*

illustration, using the space program. Is it possible to put a man on the moon? Yes, of course it is because we have already done so. If we were to start from scratch now, knowing what we know now, how difficult would it be? I say it would be *simple*, compared to the first time. The things that need to be done are known. Even you or I could do it, given time, materials, money and sufficient desire to do so. This certainly shouldn't distract from the genius and dedicated work of the scientists, but having paved the way, flights into space today are relatively routine. A century ago, telephone operators were necessary to make every phone call. Now we do it with the touch of a finger. Someday, people will roam the galaxies with similar ease. Those travelers will consider going to the moon simple. They will have other unknowns to call complex. So whether something is simple or complicated depends on how we perceive it. If we perceive it as an unknown, then we see it as difficult and are tempted to say, "I can't do it." Wise people do not know how to do everything, but they know they can learn how to do almost anything. Thus, their vocabulary does not include "I can't."

The Truth is available everywhere. It always was and always will be. It is totally fair and equal to all: black, white, yellow, green, Christian, Jew, Buddhist, Atheist, Moslem or whatever. *The Truth is the way that it is*. If we doggedly maintain some kind of denial, it can be very harsh, producing a life of darkness, fear and bondage. When you begin to understand the Truth, work with it and use it positively, then you acquire wisdom. Wisdom does not come instantaneously. But the more open and accepting of the Truth, the faster wisdom will enter your life.

One of the wisest men I ever knew was my tutor, William Penn Patrick. He constantly met the Truth head on, checking the way it was. It was quite often painful for him, especially in the beginning. He had to confront his own poverty and say, "I created this. My thoughts, my thinking did this. I am responsible." But by doing so, he gained wisdom. It may sound easy on paper, but it is probably the most difficult task anyone faces. Have you ever rowed downstream and then turned around and tried to go up? It's hard to do. The tide in most people's lives is toward negativity, failure, bondage and a need for guarantees of safety. To face the Truth and realize one is a failure, or in bondage, is to turn, face the negative tide and create success, freedom, and opportunity. It is a major undertaking, but it is also one of the great adventures.

Today, a great number of people, world-wide, are turning to face the negative tide. Many are involved with self-realization, awareness, meditation and other personal growth groups. It has become a large industry. This is an expected thing and has happened throughout history. Every 40 to 50 years we witness a form of revival, a spinning off and welling up of genuine altruism. Old dogmas are broken; new concepts challenge the old thinking. In our current generation, the various self-enlightenment movements are a result of such inner searching. Every time the consciousness is raised a little, a large mass of people become less superstitious, less fearful and more in control of their lives. They accept more responsibility for where they are personally and in so doing, gain more wisdom. These individuals recognize that they are like spiritual manufacturing plants, producing insight and wisdom to neutralize the negative chaos the world knows today. The thoughts they hold and charge with energy become reality. It isn't easy, because they are confronting the ancient and entrenched manufacturers of wars, prejudice, violence, broken marriages, battered children, and riots.

On a personal level, our products include our physical bodies, our relationships, our careers, and our role as parents and citizens. Quite often we see these as being imperfect: poverty, sickness, addictions, bad relationships. It is painful to accept responsibility because it affects our ego. Rather than taking such information in as data, like checking the phone bill, we use it instead to judge our value as a person. That is why people resist taking responsibility. The shame buttons, installed in childhood, get punched. When you take responsibility, you have to say, "I thought I had it all together. Now I realize my life is a mess. I haven't done the job right." That is a hard thing to do.

Let me give you an illustration from my life of what I mean by facing the Truth and show you how this is a reflection of wisdom. Up until I was twenty-three years of age, I had never stood before a group to speak. For all practical purposes, I was an introvert. I kept mostly to myself. Of course, I had friends and talked to people, but never before a group. If there were three, the other two conversed and I was the quiet one. I was also very careful to whom I spoke. My old programs were shame-based, as a result of being heckled for my Oklahoma accent and for stuttering. Emotionally, it was very painful and I was afraid to talk. Yet, inside I had something to say. I didn't know what it was exactly, but it had to be expressed somehow. I had a vision of a large crowd and I had something to say to them. I felt a need to get what was inside out, not for applause or power, but for self-expression. I did not know what to say, but I did know I had to speak. The recognition of the feeling and the knowing that I had to do something about it was like turning and facing that powerful tide. I realized I had been drifting in the current with the old programs and had to do something about it.

I confided in a man, who turned out to be one of those good people who really care. He talked to me about something called "Toastmasters." I said, "Yes, I'd like to try that." A couple of days later, he came by to pick me up. But he had scared me by telling me it was all professional and business people. And at twenty-three, I honestly did not think I was very "professional." The truth is I didn't feel all that good about myself anyway. I was the manager of a sporting goods store at the time, with no college degree. In fact, I had been thrown out of college. So I didn't see myself the way he saw me. He had told me about the professionalism, the speeches given and the critiques, in short, he told me too much and I was petrified. So I said to myself, "You mean I'll have to get up in front of some thirty accomplished people: doctors, lawyers and high-powered types, and t-t-talk?"

Well, he came by to pick me up, and I told him I had to work. It wasn't true; I was just desperate to avoid what I was sure would be a humiliating disaster. But we talked again, and he agreed to come by the next week. "Sure, I'll go... I really want to go," I assured him. The next week I got "sick." To make a long story short, I came up with twenty-six excuses, twenty-six weeks - six months to be exact. Every Wednesday this persistent man came after me, and every week I had a reason for not going. But I "wanted to go badly." Finally, one week he did not come by. I felt terrible, so terrible I went to that Toastmasters meeting. I sat in my car for a while and almost did not go in.

Guests were not asked to participate, so I just enjoyed listening to the other people perform. They were hard on each other. There was no such thing as a perfect presentation. Somebody would find a flaw and let them know about it. To join the club you must attend for three weeks and then give an "icebreaker" speech, that is, a five to seven-minute talk about yourself. So I did not join the club; I just went...for three or four months. They kept asking me to join, but I always had a reason. Finally, I agreed to sign up. In fact, I'd been preparing my icebreaker speech since the first meeting. I had it all written out and had practiced it in front of mirrors and while driving. I was set! The speech was seven minutes exactly. It was not the typical icebreaker though. It was philosophical, even poetic. It was written in the third person about what a certain child had experienced. I ended with page 60 of Kahlil Gibran's *The Prophet* on speaking:

> *"When you meet your friend on the roadside,*
> *Or in the market place,*
> *Let the spirit in you move your lips*
> *And direct your tongue.*
> *Let the voice within your voice*
> *Speak to the ear of his ear;*
> *For his soul will keep the truth of your heart*
> *As the taste of the wine is remembered*
> *When the colour is forgotten and*
> *The vessel is no more"*

The evening I was to do my icebreaker, an unusual thing happened. Another club was there, almost one hundred people, all strangers. I was so petrified I could not eat. In all my life this was the most terrifying moment I have known. I have had pistols held to my head and knives at my throat. I have had my throat cut open with the sharpened teeth of an aluminum comb. I've been in brawls, gang fights, fights with sharpened chains, a lot of bad situations, so fear was no stranger to me. But that night in front of one hundred or so professional people, I was quaking.

The night dragged on endlessly, or so it seemed, for the icebreaker speeches were the very last thing. Throughout the evening members vied for awards. The most coveted was the "Toastmaster-of-the-Year" award. The competition was fierce. The two clubs were evaluating each other. Finally, three hours later, totally petrified, I was called to give my speech. I do not know how I got up or moved or stood. The reality was that I gave a seven-minute talk in less than four minutes. Not once did I pause. I don't know who understood me. Blank stares were all I saw. Normally a person giving an icebreaker talks about his or her family and job. I spewed out philosophy! I got blank stares. Then the evaluation came. The evaluator, a man from the other team, was an Air Force officer, a fighter pilot. He was probably one of the most eloquent speakers I've ever heard. I think what made him so special was his kindness. I remember he said such things as, "It is refreshing to have such a poetic genius deliver such a timely and valuable message." As he went on, he made me sound downright elegant. I soaked it up.

I got active in Toastmasters and took every opportunity to speak. Actually, I became kind of fanatical. Every speech I delivered had a message. Surprisingly, by the end of the year, people were coming to hear me. Remarkably, the attendance would go up at meetings where I was a speaker. The next year I won the "Toastmaster-of-the-Year" award. I am very proud of that. It represents a change in the course of my life. I had reached a major turning point. I was ready. I quit my job and moved to Texas that same year.

Wisdom goes back to the time when I knew from inner feelings that I had to do something. And I did it. I did what made me feel better tomorrow, even though it was excruciating at the time.

The result was beneficial. I was doing those things today that feel good tomorrow.

When I got to Texas, I joined three Toastmasters clubs so I could become an even better speaker. Since then, I have become past president of three clubs. In fact, the pendulum swung too far. I never even said an "ah" (in Toastmasters it costs 25 cents each time you say "ah"). I became too polished because the professionalism, the polish, began to interfere with people's comprehending the message. They began to listen to the voice tone and watch my hands and lost the message. "What a fantastic speaker you are," they would say, "What refinement, what precision." Again, wisdom meant knowing where I was, that I was not communicating. What I did not want was applause. I did not need the strokes; I knew I was a good speaker. What I needed was to communicate what was in my gut. So I began to un-polish the professional-speaker image. Purposefully, I let "ahs" back in; purposefully, I would make mistakes. And I still do so today. I do things that in the realm of the professional speaker are not acceptable. I thank an audience or occasionally interject rough language to make a point. Communicating the message is more important to me than praise for my technique. This too is a form of wisdom. Knowing what is important and letting that predominate.

There is a tendency to confuse the thinking process with wisdom. They are not the same, nor even much related. To think is to have thoughts and ideas. Wisdom is in selecting only those thoughts which lead to a more productive life. Wisdom involves selecting, making decisions. Thinking, on the other hand, deals with data collection, organization and use. The thinking processes are:

MEMORY -- The recall of data.

ORGANIZING -- Grouping similar information together.

GENERALIZING -- Making statements about groups of data.

DEDUCTING -- Deriving facts from generalizations.

INDUCTING -- Deriving a generalization from specific data.

APPLYING -- Taking information from one situation and using it in another.

Evaluating and judging go beyond data. In these mental processes, feelings and emotions enter. A jury makes a decision from facts and feelings, as every trial lawyer well knows. Still, this is not wisdom; for wisdom implies a higher power or source of direction. Thus, the decision of the jury will be wise or not, depending on the awareness of the individuals involved.

Consider the story of the Wisdom of Solomon (1 Kings, 3). This great king's wisdom was the ability to go beyond thinking and judging to the Truth. When two women stood before him, each claiming to be the same child's mother, he did not know which one was telling the Truth. But he did know how to arrive at the Truth. He said, *"Divide the living child in two, and give half to the one and half to the other."* One woman said, "Fine, let it be done." The other said, "Oh, no, give the child to her!" By this process, Solomon knew who the real mother was, for the real mother would never allow the child to be hurt, much less killed. From this judgment Solomon became famous, not from the judgment itself but rather from the wisdom displayed:

"And all Israel heard of the judgment which the king had judged; and they feared the king. For they saw that the wisdom of God was in him to do judgment."

(1 Kings, 3:28)

Wisdom is not dependent on the thinking processes. Even the most ignorant peasant can display wisdom. However, for those trained in the thinking processes, wisdom needs to be applied at every thinking level: selecting thoughts, data and methods of organizing, then reaching conclusions and forming judgments. The degree to which wisdom enters your thinking processes will be the degree to which you display power and become a positive leader.

Wisdom is hindsight...20/20 vision...in forward motion.

We are a vessel through which this power, or wisdom, flows. It will flow through us to the degree that we open ourselves to it. The amount of water flowing through a garden hose depends on the opening of the valve. We are that garden hose. We must consciously open that valve. The amazing part is that the more we use wisdom, the greater the flow. There is no limit to the amount of wisdom. You cannot use it up!

Every human being has wisdom if he chooses to allow it to flow. All too often we know what is right, but instead we do what feels good today, or we do the wrong things out of habits and old programs. In so doing, we fail to use the wisdom within us and thus violate the Law of Use: *when you don't use it, you lose it.* The more you use wisdom, the more you get. The less you use wisdom, the less you have.

How do you get more wisdom? By using what you already have.

PSI WORLD is a vehicle to teach you how to use what you already have in a better, more productive way. That is wisdom. PSI shows you how to turn on the valve to start the flow. It is up to you to do the turning and to keep the valve open. When you know what is right and choose to go in a different direction, you are turning off the valve. For example, you know that if you drink too much, you will be ineffective at work tomorrow. You will not be creative and will feel miserable. Yet perhaps you go ahead and do it anyway. Possessing the knowledge, knowing what will happen, is not enough. Wisdom is making that conscious decision for tomorrow. Wisdom is saying, "Hey, wait a minute. That'll feel lousy tomorrow, and I choose to do today what will feel good tomorrow." The use of drugs is another excellent example of the difference between wisdom and knowledge. Drugs used in one way save lives, ease pain, and help people live fuller, healthier lives. Used in another way, drugs lead to addiction, dependence, depression and even death. Knowledge is knowing what drug to use to get a specific result. The drug addict or pusher may be just as knowledgeable as the leading physician. The wisdom of the latter, however, directs him to apply drugs only towards a positive end. Wisdom is pulling all the pieces together: the thinking processes, awareness of emotions, decision-making and choosing, in such a way as to create a better, more positive tomorrow.

All that we know of the outside world comes through perception, which is our ability to distinguish and understand by means of the senses and mental processes. Most of what we call experience is really nothing more than accumulated perceptions. But what is a perception? You see something with your eye, you feel the wet grass, you taste a lemon tart, you hear a dog bark, you smell a rose, and your mind says, "This is real." But is it? You have felt, seen, tasted, smelled and heard these things and have admitted them symbolically into your inner world. What comes into your inner world will depend on the keenness of your sensing, your attention to and awareness of detail. Thus, the perception becomes a work of art, rather than hard, fast reality. Some people's roses have white petals; others have roses with petals delicately shaded from pink to deep burgundy. The outside world is a picture painted in your inner world. You are the artist that created it. How is your picture? Is it rich in detail? Bright with colors? Exciting and full of motion? Is it unique and expressive? Or have you chosen to perceive the dull, the lifeless, and the mundane? Check it out.

A PERCEPTION CHECK

The degree to which we perceive details and notice fine points is often an indication of liking or disliking a given subject. Have you noticed how often people who are alive and full of vitality are aware of small details? Are they not the ones who remember birthdays, remember what you did or wore the last time you met? How aware are you of the details of life? The following is a short quiz to stimulate thought. The answers are not provided on purpose.

The next time you run across one of these animals, perceive it in detail.

(1) Are the ears of a cow in front of her horns, behind them, over them or under them?

(2) How many legs does a fly have?

(3) Do cats descend trees head first or hind feet first?

(4) Where is the head of a worm?

(5) Do dogs run by moving pairs of feet together, or do they move each of the four feet separately?

(6) How many toes does a robin have?

(7) Does a squirrel have pointed ears or rounded ones?

(8) Does a snake have ears? If not, how does it hear?

(9) How many fins are there on a catfish?

(10) What is the shape of a goat's head? Round? Square? Triangular? Oblong?

Your inner world (your perception) is the greatest of your works. In fact, all that you will ever accomplish can only be known to you in this inner world. The outer world exists only as you perceive it to be.

Wisdom is an inner knowing that comes directly into your inner world from the super-conscious. It is as real as an apple, a cat or a tree. Because it does not come through the five senses, which perceive only the outer world, you may have thought you did not have it. You do. Everyone does. If you accept the Trinity of Consciousness concept, then you must acknowledge the existence of your own wisdom. Wisdom springs from the super-conscious and flows through the subconscious into your consciousness and your inner world of thoughts, ideas and perceptions. If you choose to limit your inner world to only those perceptions from the five physical senses, then you will have neither the feeling of wisdom nor the peace of mind it brings. Remember, reality is what you choose to perceive and act upon as real. Acknowledge wisdom as real, use it, and you have it.

Consider the following exercise: What would it be like if you had no senses, if you were born without any of the five senses? Take a moment now and imagine what this type of existence would be like for you. Remember, you would have awareness of the super-conscious and all your inner senses. Then, one at a time add your five senses: taste first, then smell, touch, hearing and, finally, sight. Does one sense overshadow the others? For most people hearing and sight are predominant. Do your five physical senses over-shadow the inner senses? In a crowded commuter train or bus after a long day of details, how difficult it is to hear the inner voice of wisdom and, even more so, to follow it?

The conscious mind is the key. While wisdom is always there for our use, to fully enjoy its amazing benefits, the conscious mind must make the decision to allow it to appear. We must open the valve before the water will flow. But, again, if we do not use it, we lose it. The more you use it, the wiser you become. You rarely find wise persons who were instantly enlightened. Almost always it comes over a length of time and through many trials. Throughout history, nearly every time a wise person appears, whether Solomon, Disraeli, Gandhi, Nelson Mandela, or the Dali Lama, we see an accumulation of conscious decisions that have been right. Like everyone else, the wise have encountered the negative thoughts and the temptations which are actually illusions of what seems good now but will not be good tomorrow. These were the temptations of Jesus and of every man or woman who has followed or preceded him. To be aware is to have knowledge of good and evil. To be wise is to consciously choose the good.

"Talent is nothing but long patience! Go to work! Everything which one desires to express must be looked at with sufficient attention, and during a sufficiently long time, to discover in it some aspect, which no one has yet seen or described. In everything there is still some spot unexplored, because we are accustomed only to use our eyes with recollection of what others before us have taught on the subject, which we contemplate. The smallest object contains something unknown. Find it! To describe a fire that flames, and a tree on a plain, look, keep looking, at that flame and that tree until in your eves they have lost all resemblance to any other tree or any other fire. That is the way to be original."

- Guy de Maupassant, relating instructions from his teacher, Gustave Flaubert.

THE BOOK OF
FEARS

"Fear exists only in
the unknown."

Thomas D. Willhite

FEARS

"To be afraid is to have more faith in evil than in God."
- Emmet Fox

SUMMARY: Nothing stands in the way of individual progress and growth except fear. What is this emotion which so controls our lives? What can be done to counter its devastating effects? What can be done to eliminate fear? There are only seven basic fears and these are the subjects of this book.

We have all experienced fear. We have felt that gnawing inside, that sickening dread. We've encountered the loss of power and energy, the feeling of helplessness, as fear takes over. What is it, this fear? It is an apprehension of something that might happen. It is not dependent upon an actual happening. You may find you have a fear of poverty. This means you have an apprehension of being poor. You are not poor now, but you dread that state. Now, if you were, in fact, totally penniless and at the mercy of charity, you would not fear poverty nearly as much. Experiencing the state of poverty, you might dislike it, even loathe it, *but you would not fear it, because fear exists only in the unknown.*

Every leader, great or small, has had fears at some point in his or her life. So the question is not whether or not you have them but, rather, what you do with them and what you let them do to you. It's a question of, "Who's in control?" To let fear take over is to let all your energy and personal power pour into that fear. It will become so large that nothing else seems to exist. Your world will revolve around that fear. Have you not known someone whose every decision was based on fear? I know an older gentleman who hesitates to make decisions. "I've got to be sure," is his inevitable comment. Needless to say, he does not make decisions. His life just happens, with fear in almost total control. On the other hand, you can choose to be the one in charge. Faced with a fear, you can decide to march ahead even though the worst may happen and to try, even though you may fail. This is what a leader must do. This is the meaning of being a leader.

It is no weakness to have fears - only to back down.

To think is to create. This fundamental law is as valid regarding fear as it is in any other area of your life. If you think about fear and what might happen, then that is exactly what will happen! How could it be otherwise? Those pictures and thoughts you hold in your mind most of the time will materialize. You will attract what you fear most. *Worry is a prayer for something you don't want.*

The law must work in both directions, for what we desire and for what we dread, or it is not the law. If this were not so, then you would have no choice. You would have no control. There would be no freedom. Liberty could not exist. Thus, fear and adversity are necessary. Through them we can experience the thrill of overcoming and the joy of success, as well as the opportunity to grow, provided we realize they are experiences and not the final act. *Fear is an experience, not a fact.*

I like to equate "running into a fear" to "running into a stop sign." The stop sign means to stop, and then proceed with care and watchfulness. That is easy enough to do, and it makes sense. Now apply that to fears. When I find myself face to face with a fear, I "stop" and, with my inner eyes and ears, look around and see what is actually happening. Then I proceed with care and watchfulness. The fear has become a friendly reminder to pay attention.

I can identify seven basic fears: fear of poverty; fear of imperfect health; fear of pain; fear of failure; fear of loneliness;

fear of death; and fear of the unknown. Cannot all superstitions be traced to one of these? Are not amulets, charms and lucky pieces made to ease one or more of these fears? Can we not trace most strong, negative reactions to one of these seven fears? In my own life, I know I can. During the rest of this book, we will study each of these fears in depth, learning not only what it is and how it creeps into our lives, but also the practical steps to gain control. The goal is to change the fear from a barrier to a stepping stone upwards.

First, let us consider the fear of poverty. This is the fear of losing material possessions. In its extreme, and particularly in the poor nations of the world, it can be seen as the fear of starvation and the fear of having no place to live. In our modern industrial cultures, the fear of poverty shows its head as a fear of "being laid off" or a fear of being financially "eaten up" by taxes and the rising cost of living. The fear of poverty generally appears in the physical realm, but it is not limited to this. The fear of mental poverty would include the fear of losing creativity, or thinking ability; this would mean a mental starvation. A fear of spiritual poverty might be a fear of being shut off from the infinite.

It is easy to recognize someone with a fear of poverty. They cling desperately to what they have, as though their lives depended on it. Their chief demand is material security. Yesterday the news reported an incident of a man who resisted a robbery attempt and lost his life doing so. How much money did he have on his person? $4.82 and a watch worth, maybe, $25. Would he really exchange his life for something under $30? If you asked him, I believe he would not. It was the fear of poverty, and not the actual cash value, which claimed his life. What price are you paying right now to this great fear?

The Truth is, nothing you have is permanently yours. You only have possessions for the short time of your existence on earth. In reality, all things are a part of the infinite. Who can say who owns what? A hundred years from now, who will own your house or business? Not you. "But," you counter, "my children will, and I must hang on to everything for them." So I ask you again, a thousand years from now, who will own your house or business? Neither you nor your children. Do you even care? I would hope not. So why cling desperately when it imperils your very existence? I know of a couple who lived for many years in an apartment, saving for when they could own a home. The weekends were spent camping in the mountains or traveling to fascinating places. They loved to hike and explore, to watch and observe all of nature. Finally, they had enough money to buy a house. Suddenly, the weekends were spent cleaning, mowing the lawn, weeding and watering. Things neither liked to do. So what is the value of that possession? What they clung to so desperately was the very thing that denied them liberty. They were the possessed, not the possessors!

To overcome the fear of poverty is to overcome the fear of limitations. If you knew you could replace everything you might lose, would you continue to worry? Probably not. So the key to controlling this fear is to know you can recreate all that you have. Set up a savings program if you haven't already. Knowing you can start again, if need be, will give you a sense of security. Or develop alternative vocations if you desire to assure continuing income. When you realize that there are literally thousands of jobs you could fill, or train yourself to fill, how could you possibly fear poverty? It will not happen. *For those willing to work and those seeking a better way of life, there is no poverty.*

Every loss can become a powerful gain. It is all in the attitude. Early in my adult life, I had an experience, which might illustrate this point. I had worked at various jobs for several years when I decided I wanted to "try it on my own." With the help of my parents, I was able to scrape together and borrow just enough to buy a filling station. I was the manager. Dad and my brother worked in the station. It was close, but we held on, for a while, until I had an accident, which kept me out of work for many months. I could not afford to hire a manager to replace me, even temporarily. As a result I lost the station. This could have become the end of the world. I was definitely experiencing poverty! But instead of lamenting a total loss, I soon found other, more productive avenues opening. As I sit here today writing these words, I have a very clear realization: if I had not lost that filling station, I might still be there today!

As long as you personally feel you are the source of all you possess, you will have a fear of poverty. As long as you look to your balance sheet to determine your worth, you will be in danger of losing all. Only when you count wealth as your attitude, wisdom, and personal power are you free of poverty. For these three things are the ingredients which enable you to *know you can recreate all that you have.*

The next fear to consider is that of imperfect health. This would include fearing illness, physical deformity, old age and mental deterioration. Here, too, we find the fear of cancer, AIDS, heart disease and whatever other horrors which might appear. The fear of imperfect health is very common. Maybe that's why we have so much of it. As with all the fears, most people try to mask it. By denial, they think it will go away. It will not. Their actions clearly show their dread. The fear of imperfect health is seen in those who try to look and be younger than they are; in those who totally avoid any form of physical risk; in those who over-emphasize health, physical fitness, drugs and medication, and in those who incessantly talk and worry about who has what and who is in which hospital. But the strongest fear is found in people who dislike, avoid, or show prejudice towards their fellow human beings who are imperfect physically or mentally. How many times have you avoided talking to someone who is handicapped? How many times have you turned away from someone who is retarded? How much longer will you allow this fear to control you?

If you find this fear very strong with you, there is much you can do to wrestle back control. On the physical level, you might set up a balanced nutritional and exercise program. Then trust that program. If you constantly check on your health, you will only intensify your worries. You can seek out friendships with all ages and, by so doing, retain a vitality and interest in life no matter what your own age. Old age is only a state of mind. Staying current with events and styles keeps you forever in the mainstream of life. And, of course, you can learn to accept and love those who already bear the burden of physical or mental problems. They are absolutely no different from you. They want love, acceptance and happiness too. They also want to have a perfect mind and body. See them this way, and you will have mastered the fear of imperfect health. If, on the other hand, you have already found yourself with imperfect health of body or mind, then may I suggest this beautiful formula by Hubert H. Humphrey:

"As long as I have a breath of life, I'm going to try to live actively and be a part of the daily life of my family and friends, my job, neighborhood, community and country. I'm not changing my life because I have had cancer."

Substitute your own problem for the word "cancer." I know of no better recipe for living life in the face of personal handicaps than this.

Remember, too, that the source of all power, physical, mental and spiritual, is ultimately the super-conscious. This power flows through you to the degree you allow. It is a very real source of strength, energy and well-being. This is where health begins. Thus, you yourself are the true source of your own physical and mental condition. You will be as you see yourself to be, as you program yourself to be. Visualize, affirm and know you are as you desire to be.

A fundamental fact is that the infinite power, God, Spirit, Truth, Love, does not favor one person over another. One is not made greater and the other smaller, nor is one given more and the other less, neither is one made perfect and the other not. That cannot be. All are equal. All have the same rights, which cannot be denied. *You have a right to perfect health. Claim it!*

The third fear to be considered is the fear of pain. For many, many people, this is far stronger than the fear of imperfect health, or even death. The fear of being hurt physically or mentally is the basis of the trepidation about going to a dentist, the doctor, exercising, woodworking, sports, or standing up for yourself. On the mental level, it is the fear of mental anguish and wounded pride. If you fear pain, you probably know it and take great lengths to avoid even minor injuries. The overuse of medications and drugs, including the illegal use of drugs, is a symptom of a person who fears pain. The drug dulls the mind, making it insensitive. Mental anguish, so ardently avoided by modern society, includes depression, unhappiness, dissatisfaction, disillusionment and confusion.

Pain is not pleasant for anyone. It certainly is not something to be sought after. But need we fear it and let that fear control our lives? Is it wise to go to all lengths to avoid it? I think not. Pain has a valid purpose. Whether physical or mental, it is a message which says, *"There is a problem here. See to it."* Pain is the main signal that something is wrong in our lives. Without physical or mental pain, few would search for the path to growth. So when pain comes, first listen to the message. Use meditation and the various mental techniques to discover the message. Usually, with understanding, the pain dissipates. The message has been heard.

If you have experienced prolonged and intense pain, either physical or mental, you may find you have the feeling that the above discussion is too simplistic. It is too easy an answer to just "listen to the message." Is it? With all problems, are they not complex and intense while we remain in the midst of them and simple as we look back on them? *Life is not complicated, but we make it so.* Try this solution, and see what happens. The only way you can know if something works is to experience it.

Next is the fear of failure. This is the anxiety over losing face, or appearing inadequate and foolish in the eyes of others. More than any other fear, it stops progress cold. It is responsible for the inability of a person to make decisions or take risks. If you find you have been standing still in your life, look and see if this fear holds you in its grip.

The reality is that there is no such thing as failure. Let me say it again. *There is no such thing as failure. It is a state of mind, an attitude.* Failure is a way of looking at something. It has nothing to do with facts. Any experience can be thought of as a failure, if you so choose. Why not choose instead to consider all experiences as successes? For example, suppose you run for an elective office and lose. The question is, "Have you failed?" Have the people had an opportunity to express their wishes? Have you had an opportunity to express your ideas? Have the laws of the land been duly executed? If you answer "yes" to these questions, then where is the failure? Or suppose you do not score high enough on the state driver's exam to qualify for a license. Does that mean you have "failed?" Have you learned that you need to better understand the laws of the state and the rules that apply to driving? Have the people of the state been protected from having drivers on the road who do not understand the rules? Have you learned what you need to know to get your license? If you answer "yes," then where is the failure? Both you and the people of the state are better off. I would call that a success.

Usually, we apply the term "failure" to any experience in which we do not like the outcome. A politician does not like losing an election, so he calls himself a failure. A teenager does not like being denied a driver's license, so that, too, becomes a failure. Outcomes, which are "liked," are called successes. An executive likes her job, therefore she considers herself successful. A husband likes the way his marriage is going, so he calls it successful. The problem arises when we forget that it is the experience we like or dislike and, instead, consider the like or dislike as applying to ourselves. Now the outcome of an experience becomes the gauge of personal worth. This is the point of despair and depression. Perhaps you have already found yourself there.

The way out of failure begins with a separation of experience and self. You have experiences, but you are more than that. What you experience is only a reflection of where you are and have been, but not necessarily what you will become. Once you have separated the experience and the self, you can then see the experience for what it is: a growth opportunity. Whether you have liked or disliked the outcome, you have learned. Use that knowledge. If you like the outcome, use it to create other, similar outcomes. If you dislike the outcome, use the knowledge to avoid any more such outcomes. Either way you benefit. It is all a matter of attitude.

I have had so many "failures" in my life that, by comparison, your life might seem to be all successes. I have been kicked out of school and failed classes; bankrupted a business and wiped myself out financially; had a marriage totally shatter and my children refuse to talk to me (for a while). I was kicked out of Bible College as being undesirable. People have tried to kill me. There's more, but the point is I have changed my attitude since those times. I'm not proud of all the things I've done, but I do see how they have helped me be the person I want to be, by growing through these experiences and understanding my so-called failures. In essence, my happy, productive and very satisfying life is not the result of my successes, but rather the result of my failures and what I have learned from them. *Failure and success are attitudes. You choose which you display.*

Now comes the fear of loneliness. Not only is this the dread of being alone, but also of losing love, of not being liked, of rejection and isolation. People with these fears cling desperately to those around them. They are possessive of their family and friends, to the point of jealousy. Here, too, we find the person who always "tries to please" or who is always the "nice guy." People who have a fear of loneliness often fill every moment of their days with business. Their happiness depends on the acceptance and presence of others.

My heart aches for those who fear and experience loneliness, because it is an admission of a perceived separation between the conscious, subconscious and super-conscious minds. The isolation felt is bad enough on the physical plane, but on the spiritual plane it is agony.

However, for those who realize the boundlessness of the super-conscious, there is no loneliness. How could there be? Each person exists in the infinite, within and without. Nothing can be lost. No one can be separated. To do so would be to make the infinite power finite. Using the subconscious level of the mind, you can communicate with any person, living or dead, far or near. Regardless of what happens on the physical plane, the subjective communication level cannot be cut. Go even deeper, to the super-conscious level, and everything is one. Loneliness is seen to be an illusion. *Loneliness is the creation of a limited conscious mind.*

If you are by yourself, or without a love, loneliness does not seem like an illusion. It seems real. "I understand that my conscious mind is creating this feeling," you say, "but how do I stop it?" You can start by liking yourself, just as you are, with or without other people. If you like you, others will like you too. Also know that what you give, you will receive. Give love and acceptance, and you will get it back. Give companionship, and you will get that too. How many times have you asked others to share a meal, a movie or a day with you? Or are you waiting to receive an invitation first? Are you waiting for them to give before you give? If you are, it will be a long wait. That I can guarantee.

When we fear loneliness, we tend to cling to those around us and by so doing, drive them further away. Who wants to have someone clinging to them? I don't and I'm equally sure neither do you. In fact, I try to cut off those who cling, because they curtail my liberty. They drag my thoughts down and surround me with limits. Those I seek to keep around me are individually strong. Our bonds of friendship and love are made by free choice. They are bonds that do not bind, nor are they easily severed. This, then, is the way to keep relationships: *give each person freedom - including yourself.*

The fear of death includes the dread of not living and not living life fully, of being forgotten, or being unimportant. It is the fear that life has no meaning. Every day we see evidence of this fear. There are graphic accounts of deaths in papers, magazines, films and television. Billions are spent on prolonging life, often when there is no hope of recovery. Untold amounts are spent on fortunetellers, good luck charms and séances. Death is the topic at the dinner table and the research lab alike, and yet we keep it at a distance. In our Western culture we talk of the death of the man in the street or the slaughter taking place in a faraway country, yet it is taboo to speak of our own death, or that of a loved one. We visit the dying and reassure them that they will make it, when we know they will not. Why do we do this? Why do so many of us seem more death-oriented than life-oriented? Why do we always keep death uppermost in our minds and, at the same time, push it away when it gets close?

Death is an integral part of life. It is the culmination of this journey, just as birth is the beginning. There is no avoidance, no escape. You will experience death. The only question is when. Are you ready for it now? It may come tomorrow. Could you go, feeling good about your life and what you left behind? If you cannot answer these questions with an unqualified, definite "yes," then it is time to start living now, this minute, as you read these words. It is not too late; it is never too late. Five months of a life fully lived are worth far more than five, or even fifty-five years of mere existence. To live life to the fullest is the point of this book.

I believe life is more beautiful because of death. We cherish the daffodils and lilies that bloom for but a few short weeks each spring. They are more precious because they are not always with us. So it is with life. Life is dearer to us, knowing that we cannot always have it. We seek to use our time wisely, not knowing how much we have. We remember the small things: bright, sunny days, the song of a bird or the sound of a gentle rain, because we might not experience them again. This is as it should be. I am glad I do not know when I will die. I am glad I am forced by death to live each day in the now. My life is far richer because of death and so is yours. I do not fear death, nor do I seek it. I am simply ready.

What happens at death? I do not know, nor will I bore you with my beliefs and the reports of those who "almost" died. What I do know is that death is a total, individual experience. No matter what you have done in your life, no matter how heavily you have relied on others, no matter how ardently you have avoided the risks of life, *you will, through death, be forced to experience and grow on your own.* You will be forced to stand by yourself, like it or not, as all the props of material existence are stripped away. You will grow, because there is no standing still in the face of death. It seems to me that the infinite power (God, Spirit, Truth) in its wisdom is much like a mother bird. When the time is right, the young are pushed out of the nest that they may grow strong and live in freedom. Death is that push.

The infinite in its wisdom and love has forced each individual to take the next step through the mystery known as death.

I do not find it very important to speculate on life after death or to debate reincarnation. The answers will be known to us soon enough. All that we have, all that is real, is now. The issue is to live fully in this moment. That is heaven. To live in past regrets or future hopes is hell. If you would only shift your life to the now, you would know total happiness and freedom from fear. For to live in the now is to live with total individual integrity.

To live life to the fullest, live each day in total harmony and integrity.

"How do I begin?" you ask. Start with the acceptance of death. Know that you will die, as have all people, great or small. Know, too, that this is the way life is meant to be. Death is your friend. Death is a step onward. Next ask yourself, "What have I not done that I want to do?" Make a list of these things. Is there an old debt not settled? Is there an old hurt still festering? Is there someone you need to talk to? Are there affairs to be put in order? Have you taken steps to protect your loved ones when you cannot? Are there things you have dreamed of doing... some day? Do these things now and you will have begun to live. Do one more thing and you will be totally living: *know yourself. Seek out the depths within.* For those who climb the path of life in search of Truth, death is just one more step towards the goal. It is a step to be taken, not feared.

The last fear to be discussed is the fear of the unknown. I often wonder if this alone is not the basis of all fears. Perhaps the fear of the unknown is behind the fear of death, failure, illness, pain, poverty and loneliness. Perhaps all fear is really just this, the unknown.

Those who seek to maintain the status quo and those who live in traditions usually fear the unknown. It is found in the opposition to change and the clinging to the past. Fear of the unknown is subtle: "Do I always do things this way because I like to, or because I'm afraid to try another way?" Where does tradition stop and superstition begin? That you must answer for yourself.

There is a constant "known" in the universe. It is change. Nothing stays the same. Every tree, plant, rock and atom change. I will be changed by the time you read these words. You will have changed before you finish the page. *Change is the constant of the universe.* And if change is constant, then so must the "unknown" be constant. Perhaps you have lived with it so long that you do not realize that every moment of every day you face the unknown. Every day you have lived through countless unknowns. Every day you face a world where there is no total security. The security you have is the security you make for yourself. Knowing you can adjust enables you to live with changing weather and changing economic conditions. Knowing you can cope allows you to survive social upheavals. The security to face the unknown is within. There is no security in the physical world.

You must and do face the unknown. It is inevitable. Your only choice is how you face it, with resistance or with acceptance. I choose the latter. I prefer to accept and flow with the change. By so doing, I take control. I direct the course of things. I gain power. If you have studied or practiced the martial arts, you already understand this concept. The key is not to block the enemy, but to take control and use his force toward your ends.

To face the infinite unknown is the fate of man.

Seven fears control most people's lives; seven fears write the destiny of mankind. Are you one of the few who writes his own destiny? I hope so. I hope you will have the joy and thrill of waking up to a day you create the way you choose to create it. To me this is happiness, not wealth nor power nor fame, but instead, the inner strength to say, "I did it my way and am glad for it."

Fear does not enter the picture except where we let it. When we hold back and say, "I can't" or "I'm afraid," then there is a fear to be faced and overcome, not with trepidation but as a challenge. *Every fear is an opportunity to grow... every fear overcome is proof of growth.*

> *Lord, grant me the courage to walk on*
> *When adversity is around the corner.*
> *Lord, grant me the faith to walk on*
> *When the way is dark and I am lost.*
> *Lord, grant me the strength to walk on*
> *When my legs falter and my body falls.*
> *Grant me these things, Lord, and I will fear nothing.*

~ *Thomas D. Willhite*

9

THE BOOK OF LEADERSHIP

"To back down from fears, doubts and failure is the way of the follower. To face them and go on stronger is the way of the leader."

Thomas D. Willhite

Leadership

"There is much difference between imitating a good man and counterfeiting him."
~ Benjamin Franklin

SUMMARY: This book explores the dynamics of leadership: the characteristics of leaders, the differences between positive and negative leaders, the steps to becoming a leader and the various styles of leadership. Through understanding the meaning of leadership comes the answer to the question, "How do I become a Leader?" Some of you will be surprised to realize that you already are leaders; others will be shocked to learn you are not.

To be a leader is the dream of nearly every child. In my imagination I was the captain leading my men into combat against formidable odds, the knight rescuing the princess from her evil stepfather, or the daredevil race driver skidding around curves to a breath-taking finish. I wanted to be the one in charge, the one who decided, who stood out. Were not your dreams similar? Did you not also desire to be a leader? In my fantasies, I saw myself being the best, the most and the first, not realizing these things were not true leadership. One day I awoke to the reality that what I sought was an illusion. Leadership is not being the best, the most and the first. It is something else.

Now I am a leader. Not the flashy hero, or daredevil of youth, but rather a leader in the true meaning of the word. I am a leader of myself. I am also a leader of those who, of their own free choice, choose to join with me. To be a leader is to take responsibility for outcomes, good, bad or indifferent. This, more than any other characteristic or trait, is the mark of a leader.

Are you a leader now? Have you taken the responsibility for

your life, for the financial condition you are now in, for making your marriage work, for communicating with your parents, children and co-workers, for where you live and what you do? Have you taken the responsibility for being happy? Or are you saying "some-a-day"? "When I'm rich, I'll be happy; when I get married, when I feel better, when I get out of school, when I get another job, my own place, become a big shot, when - when - when..." There will be no when until you make the decision to take the responsibility and make it happen now. If you want happiness, create it now. Find the joy and beauty of this moment. Give yourself permission to be happy now. Give yourself permission to be beautiful now. Decide at this moment to be a leader, and you have become one. It can be that fast. "Taking responsibility" is not difficult. It is the "deciding to take responsibility" that is hard.

Take a moment now and look carefully at those areas in your life where you feel lack. Then take personal responsibility for them. Those lacks are there because you allowed them to be there, not because you are a school dropout, or black, or Chicano, or a woman, or poor, or overweight, or short, or can't read, or whatever! Take the responsibility for what is happening in your own life. This is where leadership begins. That others may follow you is incidental.

Leaders do not all have the same style or personality, but they do display a certain set of similar characteristics, and, generally, the more pronounced these are, the more successful the person is as a leader. Leadership is not an absolute but rather a matter of degree. Thus, each of you already displays the characteristics of leadership - to a degree.

Read through the list below and rate yourself on each characteristic, using a scale of 0 to 10.

THE CHARACTERISTICS OF LEADERS:

DEFINITE GOAL OR CAUSE: All leaders have a definite goal, or a definite cause, which they support and which is associated with them. They see this objective as greater than themselves, and commit their lives to fulfilling it. Mahatma Gandhi gave his life to freedom for India; Florence Nightingale dedicated her life to alleviating human suffering; Abraham Lincoln committed himself to a unified nation without slavery. On a scale of 0 (no goal or cause at all) to 10 (willing to totally give your life to your goal or cause), how would you rate yourself?

Self rating: _____

SELF-CONTROL: Self-control refers to the ability to keep emotions, physical desires and intellectual thoughts directed toward a given end. Often self-control is misinterpreted to mean a clamping down or elimination of feelings and desires. This is not so. Instead, think of it as a pilot would in setting his course. All the systems are used together to reach a destination. So self-control means using the power of the emotions, physical desires and intellect to move toward your life goal or destination. Emotions and desires need be checked only if they are in conflict with the goal. On a scale of 0 (emotions, physical desires and/or intellect rule) to 10 (conscious direction of emotions, physical desires and intellect toward goal), how would you rate yourself?

Self rating: _____

SELF-CONFIDENCE: This term refers to your feelings about your own capabilities. A high self-confidence indicates a strong trust in our own powers and abilities. A low self-confidence indicates a sense that power and control are "outside" and beyond your reach. People with low self-confidence frequently use the words "I can't..." On a scale of 0 (low self-confidence) to 10 (high self-confidence), how would you rate yourself?

Self rating: _____

SELF-ESTEEM: To esteem yourself highly is to approve of yourself unconditionally. A low self-esteem is to dislike or even hate the person you are. On a scale of 0 (I hate myself) to 10 (I approve of myself unconditionally), how do you rate yourself?

Self rating: _____

ENTHUSIASM: That magic ingredient which makes life exciting we call enthusiasm. It is an attitude and a feeling about life. Originally it meant to be inspired. The word derives from "ethos," which means "the God within." Now we use it to describe those people who display strong, positive, excited feelings. The 0 end of the scale is reserved for those people who act as a damper to enthusiasm. On a scale of 0 (no enthusiasm) to 10 (extremely enthusiastic), how would you rate yourself?

Self rating: _____

PERSISTENCE: The ability to stay on course despite difficulties, opposition and failures is called persistence. In a nutshell, it is stick-to-itiveness. On a scale of 0 (easily blown off course) to 10 (unaffected by even hurricane-size winds), how would you rate your persistence?

Self rating: _____

CREATIVE & IMAGINATIVE: Outstanding leaders are creative and imaginative in solving problems. (Not to be confused with being creative in the arts: painting, writing, and music.) Through them we see unique and fresh approaches to overcoming barriers. Mahatma Gandhi fought the British, and won, with passive resistance. Martin Luther King instilled pride of heritage into the civil rights movement, enhancing the image of all minorities. Golda Meir combined gentleness with raw courage to gain world respect for her people and country. On a scale of 0 (unimaginative) to 10 (extremely imaginative), how would you rate yourself?

Self rating: _____

CLEAR THINKING: People who have the ability to organize their thoughts, identify the main points and keep emotionally laden facts in perspective are clear thinkers. In times of crisis, such persons can quickly identify the problems and relevant information and get on with the business of resolving the issue. The opposite site of a clear thinker is a person whose thoughts tend to ramble. Usually, these people do not know which way to turn in a serious crisis. On a scale of 0 (clouded thinker) to 10 (clear thinker), how would you rate yourself?

Self rating: _____

ACHIEVER: An achiever gets results. All leaders get results. This is one of the primary marks of leadership. How are your results? On a scale of 0 (non-achiever) to 10 (outstanding achiever), where are you?

Self rating: _____

COMMUNICATOR: Another characteristic of leaders is their ability to communicate ideas simply, thereby influencing others. Although most leaders rely on the spoken word and personal appearances, communication is not limited to this. Helen Keller reached out of her dark and soundless world through the written word, while Joni Eareckson, a quadriplegic, started with line drawings and only later used writing and lecturing to communicate. How good a communicator are you on a scale of 0 (poor) to10 (great)?

Self rating: _____

TAKING THE INITIATIVE: Have you ever known a leader who just sat around and waited for opportunity to knock, or for circumstances to change? Instead, leaders instigate change. They start the ball rolling and alter the status quo. They are in the front where the action is. In short, they take the initiative. On a scale of 0 (drifting along with current trends) to 10 (taking the initiative), where do you place yourself?

Self rating: _____

PERSONAL COMMITMENT: Most people distinctly separate work from their personal lives. Not so with the great leaders. Their personal lives enhance and support the cause or goal for which they work. Thus, all resources are staked toward the achievement of the goal. Contrary to this are those people whose commitment is impersonal. Money and time they may give, but they do not give of themselves. The goal may be a "worthy cause" or a "good idea," but it is not a powerful personal involvement. How do you rate your commitment to your goal or cause on a scale of 0 (impersonal) to 10 (personal)?

Self rating: _____

ABILITY TO CREATE UNITY: In any march toward a goal, there will be disruptions, differences of opinion and a pulling in opposite directions. The ability to create unity behind the cause is a mark of a leader. This may require overcoming failure, settling disputes, taking criticism and/or handing it out. In short, it is the technique of keeping things in balance and maintaining harmony. How good are you in this skill area? Rate yourself on a scale of 0 (no ability) to 10 (very capable).

Self rating: _____

WILLINGNESS TO DO MORE THAN PAID FOR: Leaders reach out and do what needs to be done, regardless of what they are paid. It was not George Washington's salary that kept him at Valley Forge. Nor did Golda Meir become the Prime Minister of Israel because the job paid well. If you find yourself doing just what you are paid for, or less, then you are at the 0 end of this scale. On the other hand, if you do your job to the best of your ability, even if that means working on your own time and giving it that extra effort, then you can rate yourself a 10.

Self rating: _____

COURAGE TO MAKE DECISIONS: There is no getting around it. Leaders do and must make decisions that affect not only their own lives, but those of the people around them. The more that is at stake, the more difficult it is to take the responsibility for making the decision. Dwight D. Eisenhower, John F. Kennedy, Nelson Mandella, Anwhar Sadat have all made decisions that would affect the very existence of their respective nations. Would you have the courage to make the decisions they did? Rate yourself on a scale of 0 (avoid decisions) to 10 (can make decisions affecting lives of self and others).

Self rating: _____

After you have rated yourself on each of the above fifteen characteristics of a leader, total your score. There are one hundred fifty points possible.

TOTAL: _____

In the table on page 165, you have the opportunity to rate some of the best-known leaders. How do you compare with these men and women? The men and women I have chosen for this table are:

JESUS OF NAZARETH (c.6-c.30) -- A Jewish spiritual leader who became the founder and leader of Christianity, a religion which claims more than one-third of the world's population. Most of our knowledge of Jesus comes from the four Gospels in the Bible.

JOAN OF ARC (c. 1412-1431) -- The daughter of a provincial plowman, Joan led the French armies to victory over the English at Orleans (1429), thus enabling Charles VII to be crowned at Reims. Her skill and direction came, she said, from voices. This led to her condemnation and burning as a heretic by an English Christian church court.

ABRAHAM LINCOLN (1809-1865) -- A self-educated lawyer of the American frontier, Lincoln became the 16th President of the United States. He is known best as the leader who preserved the

Union during the American Civil War and proclaimed the emancipation of the slaves.

NAPOLEON BONAPARTE (1769-1821) -- Born in Corsica (an island off the coast of Italy), Napoleon was educated in France and became a French army officer. During the French revolution he rose to Brigadier General. He went on to command the army and declare himself Emperor of France. Under his leadership, France (temporarily) extended its domain to include vast sections of Europe and the Middle East.

BENJAMIN DISRAELI (1804-1881) -- Of Italian-Jewish descent, Disraeli was a baptized Christian. A statesman and novelist, he was twice Prime Minister of England. Disraeli led the British through critical times and established social reforms throughout the Empire.

FLORENCE NIGHTINGALE (1820-1910) -- An Englishwoman educated as a nurse in Germany. Florence Nightingale became the founder of trained nursing as a profession for women. She served as a nurse in the Crimean War (1854-1856) and received public acclaim for her wartime work. With public funds and support she started the first modern school of nursing in 1860.

ELEANOR ROOSEVELT (1884-1962) -- The wife of United States President Franklin D. Roosevelt, Eleanor Roosevelt became an acknowledged leader in her own right as a United Nations diplomat and humanitarian. Of particular concern to her were child welfare, slum-clearance projects and equal rights. During her husband's last illness, she served as his eyes and ears throughout the nation. Following his death, she served as Chairman of the U.N. Commission on Human Rights.

CHARLES DE GAULLE (1890-1970) -- A statesman, soldier and writer. De Gaulle is credited as being the architect of France's Fifth Republic (current governmental system). He led his country in exile during the Nazi occupation in World War II. Following the war, he became a political leader, and his efforts enabled France to regain its former rank in world affairs.

GOLDA MEIR (1898-1978) -- The daughter of a poor Russian Jew, Golda Meir later (1921) immigrated to Israel where she became politically active. She instigated and carried out major programs of road construction and Jewish immigration. As Prime Minister (1969-1974), she vigorously sought a peaceful settlement with the Arabs that would also guarantee secure boundaries. She served as Israel's Prime Minister during the "Six-Day War."

DWIGHT D. EISENHOWER (1890-1969) -- Commander-in-Chief of the Allied Forces during World War II, Eisenhower planned and oversaw the invasion of Europe. Following German and Japanese surrender, he commanded the demobilization of the wartime effort and worked to unify the United States Armed Services. In 1952 he became the 34th President of the United States by a landslide victory.

MARTIN LUTHER KING (1929-1968) -- The principal leader of the American Civil Rights Movement from the middle 50's until his assassination, King was by vocation a Baptist minister. In 1964 he was awarded the Nobel Peace Prize for his leadership in using non-violence in the struggle for social equality.

INDIRA GANDHI (1917-1979) -- The Prime Minister of India, the world's second largest country, from 1966-1974, Indira Gandhi led her country during times of radical changes in economics, politics and social order. Before India's independence in 1947, she was arrested and sent to prison by the British on charges charges of subversion. While there, she taught illiterate prisoners to read and write. In 1974 she was unseated and accused of misappropriation of funds.

HELEN KELLER (1880-1968) -- Although blind and deaf, Helen Keller graduated cum laude from Radcliffe College. Through her example and extraordinary accomplishments, she became a public figure and leader in the education of the handicapped.

Not all leaders raise the consciousness of mankind nor work towards the betterment of others. These I call negative leaders. There are two ways a person can become a negative leader: first, by having objectives that lower consciousness, or injure others and, secondly, by using destructive means to reach a goal (which may be very worthy). In the 20th century, Adolf Hitler is probably the easiest to recognize, along with Joseph Stalin, and any number of vicious despots and outright terrorists from (Haiti's) "Papa Doc" Duvalier to Saddam Hussein.

To determine if a goal is negative, simply ask this question, "Will it mentally or physically injure any person or group?" If the answer is "yes," select another goal! The goal itself may be valid, in fact, most beneficial. But any method or means of accomplishing a goal which is mentally or physically destructive to another, or which violates basic human rights is negative. The use of torture, deception, fears and misleading information are obviously negative.

The following are illustrations of negative and positive means:

POSITIVE	NEGATIVE
Giving	Taking
Honesty	Dishonesty
Fairness	Favoritism
Synergy	Dominating
Forthrightness	Deceptive
Rewards	Fear
Tolerance	Prejudice
Forgiveness	Revengeful
Sharing	Greed
Equality	Elitism
Praise	Degradation
Caring	Self-centeredness

Some negative leaders, such as Hitler, both have a negative goal and use negative means. Others have a positive goal but try to reach it through negative means. Fanatic political and religious groups often fall into this category.

To use positive means to strive for positive goals has been urged throughout history. This message has been available to those who understood the meaning of the written and spoken word. Unfortunately, words change with time, and what was once clear may no longer be so. The following is from a lecture I gave in Honolulu, which is a good example of what I am talking about.

"Consider the beatitude, 'Blessed are the meek for they shall inherit the earth;' (Mat. 5:5). It is also stated in Psalms 37:11, 'But the meek shall inherit the earth; and shall delight themselves in the abundance of peace.' What does this mean? What has it to do with leadership? Another reference to meekness states that Moses, one of the greatest leaders of all time, was meek: 'Now the man Moses was very meek, above all the men who were upon the face of the earth.' (Num. 123). Of all men on earth, Moses was the meekest? When I first heard that passage, I could not believe it. To me, meek meant wimpy, spineless, wishy-washy, and weak. And this was supposed to be Moses, who slew the Pharaoh's master builder with his bare hands, who took thousands of men, women, and children out of Egypt and led them in the wilderness for forty years? Not only did Moses lead his people, he provided for their safety, food and shelter. Surely he was a tough, determined and decisive leader.

"The word 'meek' had to mean something else. And it does. Traced back a few hundred years, it meant gentle, without spite or resentment and to put others first. 'Oh!' I thought, 'that makes a little more sense: blessed are those who put others first, for they shall inherit the earth.'

"Moses was strong enough to put the needs of others first. But his 'meekness' was a lot deeper than that. There is another word I use to describe Moses and most strong, positive leaders: submissive. I don't mean giving up to the whines and whims of others. I am talking about the ultimate submission to the 'will of God.' That is the submission of the conscious and the subconscious to the direction of the super-conscious. When the conscious mind and the subconscious mind work in harmony and peace, the power of the super-conscious becomes available for positive use. It is synergism in the truest sense. This was the strength and power of Moses, the true meaning of 'meekness' and the secret of all great positive leaders. *'The submissive shall inherit the earth and lead its people.'"*

Do you desire to be a leader who has integrity that people respect? I believe you do. To be a leader is natural. It feels good.

Remember, we are considering leadership of self, accepting the responsibility for the direction of one's own life. As this happens, you will, without conscious intent, find yourself in positions to lead others. People, who have a strong desire to be in command of others, generally have a low self-concept and must validate their existence through others. They seek power from without, rather than from within. This, then, is the first step in leadership: seek to become a leader of self.

The second step toward leadership is to make the decision to be a leader. Throw away the excuses and reasons you have relied on for all these years. Recognize that right now you are exactly as you have chosen to be. Accept that you are experiencing precisely what you created. This is what it means to accept responsibility. Decide to do this. Decide to be a leader.

You will know you have succeeded by the results in your life. If you desire peace but are in constant turmoil, you know you haven't made it yet. The results in your own life are the only way you can measure your growth in leadership. This, then, is the third and final step to leadership: judge by results only.

Positive leadership of others is accomplished primarily by example. "I want to be like him or her," is the ardent cry of the followers. In your own life, is this not so? Do you not want to be like the strongest positive leader you know? Thus, to rise to a position where you lead others, you must set the example. You cannot rise by destroying either those above you or those below you. Should you try to rise by such means, you will find that those above do not trust you and those below do not support you. Your leadership will, indeed, be short-lived. By setting an example, and by constantly giving recognition to those who earn it, you will gain trust and respect. By helping others to achieve their goals, you will be given support. Thus colleagues will push you up into a position of leadership because they trust and respect you. And they will continue to push you upwards because they know that, through you and your help, their own goals can be achieved. Strengthen those below you and around you and they will elevate you to leadership. You will stand on a solid base that even hard times cannot destroy. But build your base with fear, greed and promises, and even a slight wind will topple it.

Although each person will have his or her unique styles, there are two basic methods of leadership: the managerial and the charismatic. Each has good and bad points. Because of their nature, we tend to hear more about the charismatic leader. They are dynamic, active, imaginative and often just plain charming. They lead mainly through understanding people and evoking images in their supporters' minds. Because the emphasis is on people's needs and communication, there leadership frequently seems to be surrounded by disorder and confusion, ups and downs. He forces people to react and search for change. Charismatic leaders must watch that while concentrating on people, they do not lose sight of the goal. Those that support them love them with all their heart; those that hate them often do so with a passion.

Managerial leaders are rational, systematic, organized problem solvers. Their leadership directs and motivates through rewards. Although the element of excitement common to charismatic leaders may not be present here, generally you will find tolerance and acceptance. Hard work and persistence are also characteristic of the managerial leader. At times they may seem impersonal. While getting immersed in cause, the managerial leader must watch they do not neglect relationships.

The following list of characteristics will help you identify your style of leadership.

CHARACTERISTICS OF LEADERS

MANAGERIAL STYLE	CHARISMATIC STYLE
Systematic, organized	Disorganized
Planned movement	Spontaneous growth
Results and cause oriented	People oriented
Steady, hardworking	Alternating moods
Analytical	Creative, innovative
Emphasizes 'how' things get done	Emphasizes "what" things get done
Creates a sense of achievement	Creates excitement
Takes calculated risks	Takes high risks
Puts up with details	Delegates details to others
Tends to be an arbitrator	Tends to be an agitator

Should you try to become both a charismatic and managerrial leader? I think not. Rather, know the strengths and weak-nesses of your own style. I am principally a charismatic leader, so I have chosen to place around me several managerial style leaders. The balance is necessary. It is good both for me and for them. It is also good for our goal.

Every leader is also a follower. In fact, they are first of all afollower, and only through following do they become a leader. To be a leader, you first listen to and follow your own inner voice. Here is the source of direction, strength and power. What good is "per-sistence" if you are going in the wrong direction? What good is "enthusiasm" if the end is unworthy? What good is "self-control" if it leads to self-destruction? What good is any leadership characteristic if you are heading down the wrong path?

Some think to be a leader is the answer to all things. It is not. If you think you have fears now, just wait. You will have even more as a leader. If you think you have responsibilities now, you will have many more as a leader. Doubts and failures, too, may be your lot. Leaders, all of them, experience these negatives, and then conquer them. That is the mark of a leader.

To back down from fears, doubts and failure is the way of the follower. To face them and go on stronger is the way of the leader.

LEADERS AND THEIR CHARACTERISTICS

Use this space to rate yourself and other leaders you know.

CHARACTERISTICS	LEADERS	Jesus	Joan of Arc	Lincoln	Napoleon	Disraeli	Nightingale	Roosevelt	De Gaulle	Meir	Hitler	Eisenhower	King	Ghandi	Keller						
Definite Goal or Cause																					
Self-control																					
Self-confidence																					
Self-esteem																					
Enthusiasm																					
Persistence																					
Creative & Imaginative																					
Clear Thinking																					
Achiever																					
Communicator																					
Takes the Initiative																					
Personal Commitment																					
Ability to Create Unity																					
Willingness to Do More																					
Courage to Make Decisions																					
TOTALS																					

Your ratings of these people may differ from mine and other students', but probably not by very much. Note that the validity of the cause has nothing to do with the ratings. Thus, although I could in no way support any aspect of Hitler or the Nazi Movement, his ability as a leader must be acknowledged.

I interpret the totals in the following manner:

120-150 points	Leader
90- 119 points	Potential Leader
60-89 points	Average
30-59 points	Don't care attitude
0-29 points	Low self-concept (depressed)

A Leader

A leader must listen to himself...to his own inner voice of direction, strength and conviction. When this voice is not heard, he drifts aimlessly through seas of fear and doubt. When this voice is heard and not followed, he betrays himself and those around him.

A leader does have fears, doubts, failures — and conquers them. The inner voice is the foundation which holds firm against the waves of resentment and resistance.

A leader places himself aside so that the needs of others may prevail. He is gentle, strong, confident and unyielding as needed, always following the tune of his inner voice.

A leader knows fulfillment when he lives the freedom of the soaring eagle.

Thomas D. Willhite

10

THE BOOK OF POWER

"The object of the game
is to gain power and to
use it wisely."

Thomas D. Willhite

POWER

"The only limits of power are the bonds of belief."
~ H. Wilson

SUMMARY: What is this illusive thing called power? It is sought after and fought for even unto death, yet it cannot be held in your hand. Or can it? In this book we explore what power is, what it means, how to get it and how to keep it as servant to you.

The game of *power* is simply the game of *life*. All people seek power, whether or not they admit it. Power is the ability to get things done. Although not the same as wealth, power is often closely tied to wealth. For wealth can be a means to power. The rich are often skillful players of the game of life. *The object of the game is simply to gain power and to use it wisely*. However, the rules of the game are complicated and obscure. Most people get lost in the rules, or lose sight of the object. They get so tangled up in "how to gain power" that they forget why they want it and start seeking it for its own sake. They forget there is a second part to the object of the game: *to use power wisely*. This is where pleasure, joy and happiness enter. To use power wisely is the final test of leadership. Thus, the first rule, in fact the only hard and fast rule in the entire game of life is: *power must be the servant - never the master!* You are the master. You are in control. Power can only be a tool for your use and for the use of mankind.

There are three kinds of power we will address here: personal power, inter-personal power and impersonal, or spiritual, power. In a broader sense, these three powers are really the same. All power is ultimately spiritual, just as all things are part of the infinite. Infinity is incomprehensible to most, so we begin by studying the things we can observe: the flowers and animals, the rocks and streams, the moon and stars, our own bodies, feelings and thoughts. By understanding the finite around us, we begin to learn to comprehend the infinite. So it must be with power. The power which you perceive as being yours personally is, at this point, limited, because you believe it belongs only to you and is therefore finite in scope.

Self-confidence, self-esteem and knowingness wrapped up together will result in personal power. These are the ingredients from which it is created. If you feel a lack of personal power, then look to these three areas. Self-confidence is the knowledge that "I can do whatever needs to be done." It does not mean you have to do all things yourself, but rather that you can see to its accomplishment by whatever means necessary. Self-confidence also implies that you know you can learn anything you need to know, provided you are given sufficient time and opportunity. Self-confidence is built by accomplishments, particularly those that are hard to earn. Give children everything, or do everything for them and it will destroy their self-confidence; for they will not have the chance to learn that they can get it for themselves. If I were limited to but one gift to my children, it would be the gift of self-confidence, because that gift would assure them wealth, peace and happiness.

Self-esteem is the feeling that "I am good enough," not better than, but equal. Self-esteem is an intuitive feeling of self-worth, a feeling that you have an unique place in this universe. You are valuable and important...*and so is everyone else.* If you forget the last part of the sentence, the "and so is everyone else," then you are arrogant. Arrogance is the feeling that "I am better than." Some of the most arrogant people I have ever met are those on welfare because they feel that the world owes them a living. The next time you are around such people, notice how they try to make you feel uncomfortable. By attacking your self-esteem, they try to strip you of personal power. Arrogant people have power only in the eyes of those who feel inferior. They lose power in the eyes of those who do not. To build self-esteem, affirm each day that you are unique, important and necessary for this universe to function as it should. Acknowledge each day the contributions you make. It could simply be a smile, the flowers in your yard, a job well done, a kind word given to another. Though seemingly small, these are the things that make the world beautiful. Part of the poem "Desiderata" eloquently states this affirmation:

> *"You are a child of the universe,*
> *No less than the trees and the stars;*
> *You have a right to be here.*
> *And whether or not it is clear to you,*
> *No doubt the universe is unfolding as it should."*

The third ingredient of personal power is knowingness, the knowledge of the true facts of your being. To know that you know yourself and where you are is knowingness. Of the three ingredients, it is the most elusive. Just when you think you have it, you discover you do not. To achieve knowingness, you must seek for the absolute Truth of your beingness. Race, nationality, wealth and social status are ultimately temporary conditions. These things can and will change with time. The absolute Truth is that *you are.* Knowing and understanding this Truth is power. Living and being just what you are, no more and no less, is total integrity. Have you ever noticed that people with integrity have a tremendous amount of personal power? They have knowingness.

Shakespeare said:

"This above all, to thine own self be true.
And it must follow, as the night the day.
Thou canst not then befall to any man."

Take these three ingredients - self-confidence, self-esteem, knowingness - increase them in your own life and you will have a greater sense of personal power. You will feel less apart from things and more in the stream of life. You will feel a sense of stability in a varying environment. You will have a sense of being in your place, no matter where you may wander.

As I entered my teens, I had a very small sense of personal power. In that time when I should have gained confidence and a sense of worth, I experienced a sense of lack, emptiness, the disgrace of poverty and the helplessness of not being able to do anything about it. I felt rage toward a world that I thought treated me and mine unjustly. This was inside. To the outside observer I appeared confident and cocky. I was never the one to back down from a fight and no one could push me around. Often, I was silent, defiant and resentful. I had only the power others gave me out of their own feelings of weakness. I have changed considerably since that time. Now I am considered to be a powerful person, but more importantly, I know who I am and how to use my strength to benefit those around me. Without this knowledge, the struggle for power would be meaningless.

I did not achieve a powerful image until long after I had started down the road to gaining personal power. Through achievements and recognition in business and such groups as Toastmasters, I built up both self-confidence and self-esteem. At first, there were failures and much stumbling around in seeming darkness because I did not know what I was trying to achieve. Until I encountered William Penn Patrick, my tutor, I had no real direction. Then, when I came to know him and see in him the living example of what I sought, I understood the meaning and workings of power. By demanding results and accepting the responsibility for the failures and lacks in my own life, I gained knowingness. Today, I look back and find it hard to imagine the boy that I was. I still have mountains to climb, of course, but I now see them as challenges. To live is to seek challenge. I would have it no other way.

As you begin to get a sense of genuine personal power, your attitude about yourself changes. It has to. Those around you will experience this change as well, because the dynamics within you are different. You have now moved into the realm of *interpersonal power*.

Interpersonal power is the compelling influence one exercises with other people. They recognize and respect it. This is where the real power games are played. But those who lose sight of the object of the game, which is to *use power wisely*, and instead seek power for its own sake, get entangled in this area. Beware.

Have you ever noticed that when you walk into a meeting with strangers, you can usually pick out the person who has the most power? He or she may not be the person in charge, but they are in control. They have a certain demeanor. I call it the look of power. It begins with personal appearance. Step to a mirror and regard yourself, not with condemnation, but honestly, as though a good friend has asked for your opinion. How does this reflection appear to you? If it's not what you want, it can certainly be improved. To achieve a look of power, it's important to be in good physical condition, including hair, skin and nails.

It is not necessary to have a "Hollywood body," but it should be strong and vibrant within the limits of your physical build. I know a man who must wear braces and use crutches, yet he radiates a sense of physical well-being. If he can do this, how much easier will it be for those of us who have no challenges to do so? Remember, physical well-being begins first of all in mental wellbeing. Good, positive thoughts do wonders for a marred complexion and a furrowed brow. Regardless of most limitations, you can carry yourself well, even in a wheelchair. Good posture and a head held high is all it takes. When you find yourself rounding your shoulders, dropping your head or looking at the ground, ask yourself, "How am I feeling about myself today?"

Frequently, I hear people say, "If only my nose weren't so big; if only my teeth were straight; if my ears weren't so large..." I think it's great to have a prominent feature. Do not hide it or hate it, love it. It is uniquely yours. And if you truly cannot, then see about having it changed. Modern plastic surgery does miracles. All of the following celebrities are identified with a prominent feature or handicap that, with a negative attitude, could be taken as a liability:

Steven Hawking	Barbra Streisand	Randy Johnson
Andrea Boccelli	John Goodman	Bob Dole
Marlee Matlin	Mikhail Gorbachov	Woody Allen

Generally, people have more the look of power if they dress simply and with quality. Extreme fashions are often distracting. And, of course, it is much more than just physical appearance. It is a certain steady gaze, a quiet body and relaxed hands which subtly say that you belong right there, right then.

This look of power is natural for some, but not most. It can be learned through practice. With a mirror, or on the screen of your mind, see yourself as confident and relaxed, yet present and alert. Remember, the look of power is a look you control.

The members of an office or family group have varying amounts of power. Some are virtually magnetic, while others fade into the background. Where do you fit in? Are you at or near the center of power? Or are you one of those lost in the background? Are you happy where you are, or do you want to move closer to the center of power? Or away from it? Why? The answers to these questions form the very heart of your interpersonal power relationships.

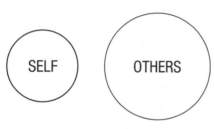

The "smaller-than" feeling

How big you feel in relationship to another person is something I call your "psychological size." If you feel "smaller than" most of the time, then you have very little power in relation to others. In essence, you are giving all your power to them because of a low self-concept or low self-esteem. The diagram on the left illustrates this feeling. You perceive others as being smarter, wiser, more intuitive and more *powerful*.

If you often feel "larger than," you are seeing yourself as being psychologically bigger than others. You feel smarter and wiser and *more powerful* than those around you. You see others as being weak and indecisive. Others describe you as arrogant or egotistical.

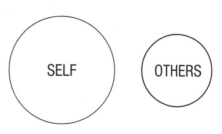

The "larger-than" feeling

To show a feeling of equality with others, you would use two equal-sized circles, such as here.

The "equal" feeling

To understand our power position in our work or family setting, we can use the concept of psychological size through different-sized circles.

Begin by drawing a circle to represent yourself. Then draw circles to represent each person that is considered a part of your family (or work) group, whether or not they are physically related. Draw the circles so that everyone gets a circle roughly equivalent to his or her relative power. Next, draw lines of power of varying thickness to indicate dependency, obligation and close-ness. A double arrow would indicate mutual exchange of friendship or confidence, while a single arrow points to a dependency/control situation. The following illustrated family group

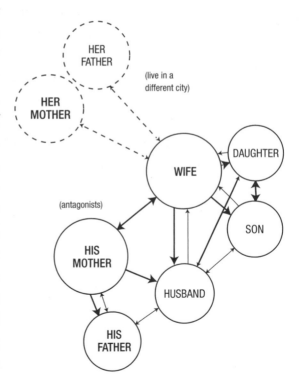

is of a husband and wife who found it difficult to break the husband's parental ties. Their marriage was under considerable strain, yet neither could say exactly why, until they started to look at the power relationships.

In this family group, the power is held by the wife and the husband's mother, who are somewhat antagonistic toward each other. The husband is the pawn in the middle of the power play between wife and mother. No one is happy with the situation as it currently stands. Although there are several ways to go from here, the easiest would be for the husband to increase his personal power by means already discussed. By so doing, he will cause a shift in the power relationships above.

Diagram out your own family relationships according to power. Save it. Several months from now, after you have had time to build your own sense of power, repeat this exercise and compare the results with your original diagram. You will be amazed to see the differences and shifts of power which have occurred.

The point of a power chart is to understand the control of an organization. It may clearly illustrate how decisions are made and implemented. If you feel like an "outsider" in your work setting, it is probably because you are not involved in the stream of power. The chart can be used to identify the key people who can bring you into the flow, or whom you need to include as you build your own power structure.

The key to increasing power within an organization is to expand your responsibilities and duties. Whereas most employees are trying to avoid jobs and added tasks, one might consider taking on more work than they can possibly do. Very soon they will probably need the services of an assistant; the need will be obvious to all. In essence, you have created a new position for yourself; one

The same technique can be applied to your work setting, as illustrated below. I started with the following organizational chart of P.S.I. Inc.:

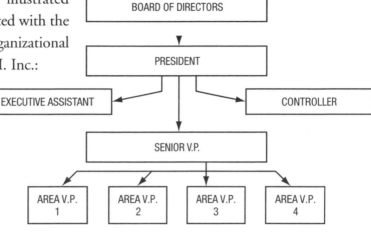

Then, by using differentsized circles and lines, Itransformed it into the following power chart:

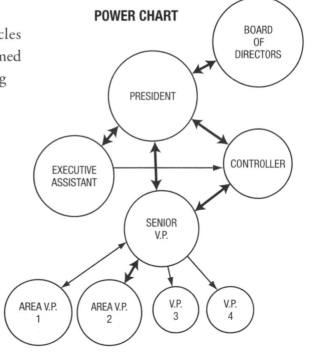

where you are in charge of seeing that certain tasks and jobs are accomplished. Continue to do this over a period of time, and you will find yourself the head of a section. In contrast is the person who tries to "climb up" to the top. In order to move to a higher position by climbing, it is necessary that there be a vacancy up top. And that can be a very, very long wait.

In expanding, there are two rules to keep in mind. The first is to *delegate without giving up responsibility*. This means you accept the responsibility for accomplishments without actually doing the legwork yourself. Needless to say, this is a high-risk position. You must trust your subordinates to follow through on your directions. Good communication skills, frequent progress reports and careful selection of personnel are the ingredients of success. The second rule is to *replace yourself with someone who can do your job better than you can*. If you are moving upward, someone will have to take over your job. Replacing yourself with someone who does poor or mediocre work, will cause you to constantly redo, or closely supervise the work. In the extreme, you may even find yourself back in your old job. On the other hand, if the new person can do your old job better than you ever did it, there is no way you can slide back down. You will be securely entrenched in your new position and ready to continue your expansion upward.

In either family or work, time is power. Whoever occupies most of your time has extensive power over you. By denying others your time, you exercise power over them. Arriving late, delaying meetings and being pressed for time are all negative power moves. Your awareness of these strategies will enable you to counter them and actually turn them into your advantage.

Recently I was scheduled to attend a meeting which began

at 8:00 a.m. Since I was flying in, I had the organizer of the meeting arrange for someone to pick me up at the airport. Due to "miscommunications," I was picked up an hour late and arrived well after the meeting had started. Understanding the power play involved, I was able to turn it around by simply stopping the meeting and requesting a complete recap of all that had been discussed. Thus, instead of losing power through the incident, I gained it.

No discussion of interpersonal power would be complete without a mention of sexual signs and maneuvers to gain power. Office flirtations are frequently carried out with just such an end in mind. Fortunately, both sides generally realize the intent and that it need not be followed up. Breaking the pattern is a successful way of shifting power. My wife is an expert in this field. Confronted with even a subtle sexual maneuver during business negotiations, she will acknowledge the ploy with a nod then proceed to ask, with seemingly perfect innocence, the most direct and pertinent questions concerning the matter at hand. Needless to say, she is perceived as being an extremely powerful woman by men and women alike.

To be aware of power moves and games is a good thing. To be involved in them is of questionable value. Gaining power over people can be as intoxicating as alcohol and drugs and is totally compatible with sex. But like most intoxicants, it dulls the senses. Too much of it diminishes one's perspective rapidly. Power becomes the king and the players are the slaves. The first rule of the game, *to use power wisely*, is forgotten. Francis Bacon said, "*It is a strange desire to seek power and lose liberty.*" But this is exactly what those who love power do.

The women and men with the greatest strength do not play

these games. They recognize that all true power, including their own sense of personal power, is actually impersonal in nature. It is in all things. It is limitless. Why squabble for power when there is more than enough to go around? Why fight for what is available to all? Why worry about position, when one's true position in this universe is understood and secure?

Impersonal power is power in its essence, the source of all life. Nature and all that is in nature, including you and me, is but the manifestation of the living power. Yes, I mean you specifically, you who are reading these words. You are a focal point through which power flows into this earth experience. The energy you experience as yours, in reality, is yours only for a moment in time. It is a part of, and always connected to, the infinite. It includes all things. *The living power is in you just as surely as you are in it.*

You have a choice. You can either flow with this power or struggle against it. The latter is to fight a losing battle. How clearly I learned this lesson as a young man. Long before I began to search for myself, I had been taught this fundamental Truth. It happened on a beach in Southern California. I strayed too far from the swimming area and found myself caught in an undertow. It was a frightening feeling to experience the power of the ocean and know I was totally in its control. At first, I struggled madly to reach the surface. I fought the current with all my strength, but still it held me in its grip. I felt my lungs would burst. Then I remembered someone telling me in the past that when you are caught in a riptide or an undertow, relax and swim with the current to safety. So I did. Moments later I broke the surface. The ordeal had passed, but it is still as vivid to me today as it was on that sunny summer day many years ago. Isn't it strange how small incidents carry such big messages? In less than a minute and a half, I had experienced a universal Truth: *You can either be in harmony with this power, or you can struggle against it, but there is only one way to reach the top.*

The impersonal living energy is the source of all power. Understanding impersonal power gives total self-confidence. Since this is infinite, you can do all things. Make this affirmation: "Given sufficient time, I can understand and do all things, be it quantum mechanics, nuclear physics or the most complicated mathematical formula. With time I can become a great surgeon or a brilliant artist. And if I choose to do any of these things, or find that I need these skills or knowledge, then *I will be given sufficient time.*" Understanding impersonal power brings complete self-esteem. Since your source of power is the same as everyone else's, how can one person be better or stronger than another? How can I dislike myself or feel "less than" when we draw from the same source? Does my little finger feel "less than" the other fingers because it is smaller? Does the skin on my hands feel "less than" because it is not the same as the skin on my face? No. Likewise, you are equal to everyone else on the face of this planet. We spring from the same source. Understanding impersonal power gives knowingness. Since your source of power is the only one that exists and is, in fact, all inclusive, you have discovered the absolute Truth of your being. You are a manifestation of infinite power.

You are impersonal power.

Power was defined at the beginning of this book as the ability to get what you want and the ability to get things done. You might be wondering exactly how impersonal power fits into this definiton. "How does 'impersonal power' mean that I get what I want and need? How does it help me to get things done and get where I want to go?" That is a fair enough question.

Visualize that your arms are outstretched with a piece of twine in each hand. At the end of each string is an iron ball. Feel their weight. Become aware that they are equal, exactly the same size, color, texture, everything, except the iron ball in your right hand is magnetized. It displays a force that attracts other objects made of ferrous materials (iron). In a magnetized object, the molecules are oriented parallel to each other so that the force of each molecule is moving in the same direction. As a result of the combined forces of the millions of molecules, the object displays the attraction force we have named magnetism.

In the above description of magnetism, the key word is *displays*. The object displays a power or force. It neither generates nor creates it. So one ball displays power; the other does not. One ball is internally aligned; the other is not. In all other respects, they are identical. They are made up of the same kind of molecules. They have the same exact potential. All that is necessary for the display of power is the alignment of molecules.

Let's translate this into our lives. Ever since we were small children, we have heard such things as, "Johnny is a musical genius. Susan has a low IQ. She's special. Karen is artistic. Joe is clumsy. Mike doesn't have what it takes to make it in life. Sally doesn't have a head for figures." Almost all of us have heard statements like this. Perhaps some of them have been used with your name attached. Do you really think, down deep, that these statements are fact? Do you think God, that infinite power or spirit, is prejudiced? That all the good things are given to some and not to others? I thought we were all equal. I thought we all had the same access to infinite power within. There are people who would like us to believe that some are fated to an easy, favored life and others to a hard one. *That is a lie*! The reality is that "the molecules are aligned" in one individual and not the other. One individual displays the power or talent; the other does not. One attracts what they desire; the other does not. One is able to do what they want; the other is not. One is internally aligned; the other is not. *There is no other difference.* Each has the same make-up, the same energy and the same potential. All that is necessary for the display of power is the alignment of molecules.

This is not about aligning physical molecules; it's about the alignment of thoughts. The "alignment of molecules" is the comprehension and digestion of the concepts which we have been studying here. Throughout history, all the great teachers of life have presented these same concepts. This is not new information, it is just offered in a different way.

The "alignment of the molecules" is learning, discovering and experiencing win-win relationships that are beneficial to all concerned. It is using the screen of the mind and actually experiencing that *to think is to create*. Alignment means the I AM concept is applied. "Meekness" is understood as being submissive to the infinite super-conscious mind. It is being strong enough to put others first. The more we comprehend the Trinity of Consciousness, and using that understanding to Mastermind, our thoughts and actions come into line with these universal Truths, and the more power we will display. These concepts bring both liberty and power. A conference in Geneva will not free mankind. A treaty among all the nations of the earth will not guarantee peace. A nuclear bomb does not make a powerful nation. No one individual or nation can liberate a people. Only individuals can free themselves. *Only your thinking can free you, because you will always choose the way you think.* Nobody will choose for you, unless you allow them to do so. And even that is a choice.

THE CONCEPTS GIVE YOU FREEDOM.
THE CONCEPTS GIVE YOU LIBERTY.
THE CONCEPTS ARE POWER.

11

THE BOOK OF LIBERTY

"Liberty is the ultimate goal of this life experience."

Thomas D. Willhite

LIBERTY

*"The human race is in the best condition when it has the
greatest degree of liberty."*
~ Dante Alighieri

SUMMARY: *Liberty is the ultimate goal of mankind. The formula for
achieving liberty has been given over and over again throughout recorded
history. In the Bible, for instance, it appears as the Four Horsemen of the
Apocalypse, the Four Beasts of Revelation and in the Gospels of Matthew,
Mark, Luke and John. Yet few have heard the message. Listen deeply as it is
said one more time.*

If you were granted one wish, and only one, what would it be?
Wealth, power, wisdom, love, liberty? What you choose to
concentrate on with all your mental power, will, in fact, be created.
So choose carefully. This is not a flight of fancy; *it is reality*.

For me, there is only one thing I truly want above all others and
that is liberty. This is the ability to be the conscious architect of your
environment, your experiences and yourself. You alone are in control
and responsible for what you create. This is what I desire most. I
believe *total liberty for all mankind is the goal of this earth experience*.

I haven't achieved total liberty, yet. But, by practicing the
principles contained in the concepts, my wife and I have grown so
much. We have manifested many of the material things we want:
condominiums in resort cities, airplanes, luxury cars. Notice I did
not say that we owned all these things. Rather we "have" them; we
"have the right to use" them. Some things we do own of course,
but not everything. Ownership is not necessary. For example, if
I have the use of a yacht anytime I wish, what does it matter if
I own it? Liberty does not depend on material wealth. Rather, it

- 186 -

is the power to have what you want when you want to have it. Ownership of the things is immaterial.

Through following the concept of rendering service to others, we have been able to expand our lives. We often travel to various parts of the world, meeting fascinating people, making loyal friends and taking part in the positive changes of our time. This is not the result of political power but, instead, the result of responsible personal power. Many people confuse "freedom" and "liberty." Freedom is the right to choose among alternatives. In reality, everyone has this freedom. For some people, however, the consequences of their choices are out of proportion. If by choosing not to work, a person forfeits his life, then, although he has the freedom to do so, it is rather limited. We generally use the word "freedom" to mean the right to choose when the consequences for choosing are proportionate to the choice. Liberty, on the other hand, is the power to do and be as you please. Whereas everybody has the freedom to choose, few have the liberty to do and be as they please. This is because *liberty is always self-earned*. It is the result of the choices you make. No one can give you liberty. You must create it yourself.

One of the most effective paths to liberty is through an understanding of the nature of man. This has been available since the beginning. It has been passed down in a variety of symbolic forms. Symbols are used for two reasons. First, the mind works in pictures and images. So symbols have greater and deeper impact than words. They make it easier to recall the totality of a concept. Secondly, symbols are not dependent on language, or the degree of awareness. Thus, the same symbol can have meaning to people who speak different languages, as well as those who are at vastly different levels of spiritual development. The truly important knowledge has always been conveyed through symbols.

The nature of man has been revealed in any number of symbols, from the hermetic mysteries of the zodiac, to a dove as a symbol of our yearning for peace. The Four Horsemen of the Apocalypse is a powerful symbol that is particularly relevant to our modern world and is useful in understanding how to achieve liberty. The Four Horsemen stand for the four natures of man: the physical, the emotional, the intellectual and the spiritual. This is our makeup as we currently experience life. There will come a time when the physical, emotional and intellectual will be transmuted into the spiritual. Then we will know, not just believe, that the spiritual is all, and the only reality is the universal power, the I AM. Until that time, we must deal with the four natures which the Bible calls the Four Horses. They are the Pale Horse, the Red Horse, the Black Horse and the White Horse.

The Pale Horse represents the physical nature of man. "Pale" is a color without description, a grayish, ashen color. It is the word we use to describe a person who is ill or fear-struck. It is the color of terror and the dread of death.

And I looked, and behold, a pale horse: And his name that sat on him was Death, and Hell followed with him. And power was given unto them over the fourth part of the earth, to kill with sword, and with hunger, and with death, and with the beasts of the earth. (Rev. 6:8)

The rider of the Pale Horse lives in the physical realm, subject to disease, death, war, famine and suffering. Knowing only the physical, which must with time perish, his lot is a living death and hell on earth. Unpleasant as it may seem, a large number of people ride this Pale Horse.

People who ride the Pale Horse live for physical sensations: eating, drinking, drugs and sensuality. Addicts of all descriptions, including sexual perverts and chain-smokers all ride the Pale Horse. The obsession with pleasures of the body controls their decisions. They fear old age, for to them it represents decrepitude, pain, emptiness and decay. However, the Pale Horse does not refer just to the physical body. It refers to all physical and worldly things. Thus, those who seek above all else money, position, power (for its own sake) and material honors also ride the Pale Horse. The workaholic, the power-hungry and the sensationalist all sit on the Pale Horse, as well as those who strive for riches, recognition and influential friends. A person who seeks office in order to serve others is not on the Pale Horse. Neither is one who has unlimited wealth and uses it wisely for the benefit of others. Nor are those who are ill or handicapped and do not dwell on their condition. It is not the circumstance but rather the mental attitude which determines *the Pale Horse rider. The Pale Horse rider lives and thinks in the physical realm.*

The Red Horse represents the emotional or feeling nature of man. The color red elicits emotions. It is the color of fire and passion. And this is the nature of the Red Horse rider:

And there went out another horse that was red: and power was given to him that sat thereon to take peace from the earth, and that they should kill one another: and there was given unto him a great sword. (Rev. 6:4)

The rider of the Red Horse is the person who lets his emotions control him. This is the one who gets angry over trivial things, who reacts to newspapers and television. A Red Horse rider will have violent feelings about politics, religious doctrines, or social mores and yet often have little knowledge of these things. Temper tantrums, prejudices, childish behavior and controlling other people's lives are indications of a person on the Red Horse. Strong emotions alone do not necessarily indicate a Red Horse rider. Strong, directed emotions can be a very positive thing. They are the power that moves you towards your goals, sees you through the rough times and pushes you to success. Undirected, these same emotions lead down a path of self-destruction. Most people who lack, or suppress emotions are Pale Horse riders at the mercy of physical circumstances and environment. The Red Horse riders have strong emotions which run away with them. The Red Horse riders are controlled by their passions and obsessions. In this world there are many Red Horse riders.

Black is the color of the intellect, factual knowledge, reason and cold logic. The Black Horse represents the intellectual or mental nature of man.

And I beheld, and lo a black horse: and he that sat on him had a pair of balances in his hand. And I heard a voice in the midst of the four beasts say, 'A measure of wheat for a penny, and three measures of barley for a penny': and see thou hurt not the oil and the wine. (Rev. 6:5-6)

The pair of scales held by the Black Horse rider represents lack or famine. There is not enough to go around; it must be measured and rationed. The Black Horse riders are those who let the intellect dominate their lives to the exclusion of their emotional, physical and spiritual natures. These must starve so the intellect can prevail. In comparison to the Pale and the Red Horse, very few ride the Black Horse - yet some do. Atheists, intellectuals and those who demand a reason for everything are often riding the Black Horse. These demand that everything about mankind and nature be explained precisely in words and fit into the patterns and limits they set. They deny the spiritual without even knowing they do so.

Having a good intellect has nothing to do with riding the Black Horse. The intellect is a valuable tool. It is what you are using now to understand these words. We use it to secure the things we need and want. Without brilliant intellects we would not have roads, planes, bridges, buildings, books, phones, high quality produce and all the other conveniences of the modern world. The intellect is good, desirable, needed and positive. Only when we make a "god" out of the intellect does it become destructive. The intellect can deal only in the physical realm. It knows not wisdom nor can it comprehend the infinite. When the intellect is held above all else, then we ride the Black Horse. *The Black Horse rider is dominated by the intellect.*

The last is the White Horse, representing the spiritual nature of man. In this horse lie the solutions to all problems.

> *And I saw, and behold, a white horse: and he that sat on him had a bow and a crown was given unto him and he went forth conquering, and to conquer. (Rev. 6:2)*

This horse, which is the color of purity and light, goes forth to conquer. Riders of the White Horse must realize and demonstrate the infinite power, the I AM power, the universal mind, God. This must be first in their lives, for the White Horse is the spiritual aspect of us all. To put this infinite power first means to become totally in tune with the super-conscious, to put aside limits, to know and trust your inner voice. For those who do this, the reward is a crown (victory) and a bow (accomplishment). *The White Horse rider puts the spiritual first.* Very few, indeed, ride this horse.

Which horse are you riding? Pale, Red, Black or White? The answer is evident by the results in your life. Do you suffer from health problems, poverty, a feeling of discomfort or loss? If so, then you are riding a Pale Horse. Does your life seem out of control with lots of ups and downs, torn feelings and depressions? If so, then you are riding the Red Horse. Is your life a disillusionment, a disappointment, where there seems to be no meaning? If this seems to fit, then you ride the Black Horse. Is your life a life of liberty, full of health, wealth and peace of mind? If "yes," then you ride the White Horse. You may argue that your life doesn't exactly fit any of these descriptions. And you are probably right. You may find that throughout your life you switch horses. You may find that you ride all of the horses somewhat. The question is which one do you ride predominantly? Identify that horse, and you can locate the key to unlocking your potential. The story of the Four Horsemen of the Apocalypse shows the way to liberty. If you want health, happiness, prosperity and, above all, liberty, *you must ride the White Horse; there is no other way.*

How do you get off a Pale or a Red or a Black Horse and onto the White one? Must you deny all material pleasures and totally control the emotions and subjugate the intellect? Certainly not. Such action would only enslave you further. The key to riding the White Horse is in the description of the White Horse rider: *the White Horse rider puts the spiritual first.* The "spiritual" means the super-conscious, the inner voice, the universal power of good. White Horse riders do not deny the physical, emotional, or intellectual; rather, they direct them according to their own inner voice toward the benefit of all mankind. They seek a higher goal, one beyond the three-dimensional plane of the physical world we know. Thus, physical pleasures are sought not for their own sake but as a tool to a greater goal. Wealth becomes a means to an end. The emotions, and they usually are very strong ones, add vitality, energy and commitment. From the intellectual nature comes the practical knowledge to put it all together, plans, follow-through, alternatives, evaluations and decisions. This way, the energies and goals of each of the three natures are transmuted to the higher spiritual nature. In so doing, the White Horse comes forward. You become a White Horse rider. *When the Pale, Red and Black Horses pull together, equal in balance and strength, towards a worthy goal, then the White Horse will emerge.*

Consider for a moment some historical figures who rode the White Horse during at least part of their lives: Buddha, Jesus, Lincoln, Nelson Mandella, The Dali Llama, Florence Nightingale, Albert Schweitzer, Martin Luther King, Bill Wilson, to name only a few. Actually they were quite alike. They all had a dedication to the betterment of mankind and fully committed their physical, emotional and intellectual natures toward the achievement of that goal. But do not think that becoming a White Horse rider will require you to be a martyr, or a national leader. There are many White Horse riders whose names are unknown, whose accomplishments go unrecorded. It does not make them less than the others. In any case, all earthly glory eventually fades. A thousand years from now, many of those listed above will be all but forgotten.

Right now, Western civilization as a whole is riding the Black Horse. With the Renaissance came the discovery of intellect, followed by an emphasis on science. Our educational systems and social and political institutions reflect this intellectual dominance.

It has not always been this way. In the Middle Ages, Western society rode the Red Horse into the Crusades and other vainglorious adventures. Rome fell because it rode the Pale Horse.

Today, our civilization has the opportunity to ride the White Horse. The emphasis on humanism and awareness indicates the time is ripe. It is my goal to see that this happens.

Peace of mind and liberty in our time.

The table below lists several of the other references throughout history to the four natures of man. We have presented only a bare suggestion of meaning and interpretation. Most of the search we leave to you, if you choose to do it. Through searching you will command an even greater understanding of yourself and your four natures.

The "Peace of Mind Square" is another way to illustrate the four natures of man. The sides represent the physical, emotional, intellectual and spiritual, respectively. They are joined to form a square, each side being of equal length and importance. When this happens, peace of mind results. Should one side be too short or too long, then no square can be formed and less peace of mind will be achieved. The steps to the Peace of Mind Square are blocked by envy, hate, jealousy, limits, hurt feelings, fears, etc. These are the result of riding the Pale, Red or Black

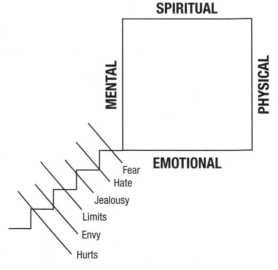

Horse. Peace of mind is the result of riding the White Horse. No matter how it is said, there is only one way to health, happiness, joy, peace of mind and liberty. The choice whether or not to follow the path is yours.

In the Peace of Mind Square, as well as in the Four Horsemen of the Apocalypse, maintaining equality between the physical, emotional and intellectual is essential. If there is no balance, then one must predominate. Only with all three pulling together in one direction, mutually supporting each other, can the spiritual emerge and gain control. For a life to be truly successful,

THE NATURES OF MAN

SOURCE	PHYSICAL	EMOTIONAL	INTELLECTUAL	SPIRITUAL
Bible: Book of Revelation, Chapter 6	Pale Horse	Red Horse	Black Horse	White Horse
Bible: Book of Revelation, Chapter 4 (Four Beasts)	Calf	Eagle (transmuted from the scorpion/snake)	Beast with the face of a man	Lion
Bible: The Four Gospels	Matthew	Luke	Mark	John
Bible: Daniel, Chapter 3	Shadrach	Meshach	Abednego	Fourth form in the furnace
Bible: Book of Numbers - The Tribes of Israel	Reuben (South)	Dan (North)	Ephraim (West)	Judah (East)
Elements of the Ancient World	Earth	Water	Air	Fire
The Zodiac	Taurus	Scorpio	Aquarius	Leo
Egypt - The Sphinx	Animal Body	Wings	Human Face	The Ankh, sacred symbol on the forehead

this balance must happen because the super-conscious is the source of all power. All life and consciousness begin in the spiritual and, in reality, never leave. The senses deceive us. We see a tree or an apple and forget the life force needed for its being. To bring your life into balance means to get things back into perspective based on spiritual awareness. This is to acknowledge the rightful place of the physical, the emotional and the intellectual in your existence. By so doing, you gain power, peace of mind and liberty. *Balance is the key to power.*

Consider the modern world in which we must live. What will it be like as you work to create liberty in your life?

You will find that some people resent you. It is important to know ahead of time that you will meet resentment and resistance on the road to liberty. As you put your life in balance, you will begin to achieve goals. Your life will have purpose and vitality. Those close to you, both at home and at work, will notice the difference. Some will support you as you change. These are your true friends. Others, unfortunately, will resent the change because they feel threatened. You have changed the rules! Still others will respect the results in your life but won't like you anymore because you will appear to be somehow better than they feel they are. They will probably respect you, but they will not like you. However, for every friend that fades away, rest assured a new and stronger one will appear. For just as some people can no longer relate to the changed you, others will be drawn by the changes in you. *There is balance in all things.* If something is taken away, an equal amount will be returned to you. It is only the form in which it returns that is unknown.

Be prepared, too, for the loudest and strongest criticism to come from those nearest and dearest. They will be the first to notice the change and not know how to cope with it. Here I speak of your parents, your spouse and your children. Especially your children. Their criticism is not of words but of hurt looks, anger and tears. Think how you would react if, suddenly your parents made a major change in their lifestyle. When a child's world, so newly built, is suddenly changed, they see it as shattered. It may be necessary to start over and build a new relationship. I know from personal experience that it can be painful. There was a point in my life, perhaps you will recall it from my personal story, where I knew I had to change, to go on at the direction of my inner voice. Yet I also knew that my beautiful children did not understand. My heart was torn. For their sakes and mine, I did go on to be all that I could be. My love for them would not permit me to do otherwise.

At this point, you might be asking yourself, "Can I achieve liberty and stay married?" The answer is definitely *yes*, if you want to. But it takes work and commitment.

I have a beautiful wife. She is the most capable, confident and powerful woman I have ever known and she is totally feminine. She does not try to be like me in any way. Jane is completely herself. I could not ask for a better supporter, still she has liberty as do I. A marriage in which each partner experiences liberty is beautiful. I wish you each such a relationship. Many see liberty as a shining pot of gold at the end of the rainbow. They think that with liberty all troubles will vanish and the days will flow without care. This simply is not so. Liberty is a state of mind, which will be reflected in the material world in terms of health, wealth and power. There is nothing said about freedom from troubles, in fact, you will have more and bigger ones than you do now. For the stature of a person is gauged by the size of the problems he or she handles. As you achieve liberty, you will also gain the ability to deal with the problems you face. The balance of the universe is maintained. Kahlil Gibran wrote:

> *You shall be free indeed when your days are not without a care nor your nights without a want and a grief, but rather when these things girdle your life and yet you rise above them naked and unbound.*

And so it will be with you. There will come a time when you realize troubles are but passing shadows. Then you will know you have indeed achieved liberty.

My personal dream is to help the people of the world attain peace of mind and liberty in my lifetime. Or if I should not see it in my lifetime, then that my children may. For I know that *liberty is the ultimate goal of this life experience.* It is our birthright, waiting for us to claim it. Go forward now and claim yours.

12

THE BOOK OF VISIONS

"The trouble is not in changing thoughts but in keeping thoughts changed."

Thomas D. Willhite

VISIONS

*"Where there is no vision, the people perish: But he that keepeth
the law, happy is he."
(Pro. 29:18)*

*SUMMARY: There are only two ways to go through life - one positive
and the other negative. The principles remain constant. It is how we apply
them that differ. I saw this illustrated clearly in a vision, a vision which
then went on to become the PSI dream. In this book I tell of the vision I
saw then and the one I see now. It is a vision of a life more complete and
beautiful for all.*

From the beginning, human beings have experienced dreams and visions that are filled with symbolic images. Legends and parables are symbolic by nature. They have been handed down since ancient times. Many people today view them as fantasies, the mental wanderings of those long dead, which can be a mistake. Prophets and oracles have influenced the history of nations since before Biblical times.

By the term "vision," we mean a revelation of a Truth. Visions are not limited to prophets and enlightened masters. Almost everyone has had some kind of visionary experience. The problem, of course, is that many do not recognize them for what they are. To be sure, some of them are dramatic, but for most of us, the sky does not open and angels with trumpets do not appear. Generally, we are given a subtle nudge down the right path, or an encouraging glimpse of future possibilities. Often it's a whispered warning. The problem is our receptivity. Are we willing to pay attention? We ignore these messages from our Higher Selves at our peril. How often have we experienced some unpleasantness and exclaimed, "I knew that was going to happen! I should have listened to myself!" Yep.

There is another sort of vision, the kind we create ourselves, when we conceive a project and begin to "see" it on the screen of our mind as completed in all its details. We also create visions for the way we want to live our lives. PSI itself began as a vision. The concept was to offer people a method to achieve a positive way of life. The PSI workshops, seminars and activities are simply a vehicle to transport one from the years of fear-filled confusion which dominate most of our lives, to a way of living where we can enjoy the liberty of self-confidence, security, spiritual growth and the realization that our lives make a positive difference in the world.

Specifically, the PSI life is based on results. This is the first key to keeping yourself on the positive path. Only the results in your own life can give you an unbiased picture. *Judging by results is often harsh, but always fair.*

The second key to a life of growth is to personally accept the responsibility for those results. They were not done for you or to you. Consciously or unconsciously, you are responsible for all your experiences, pleasant or otherwise. So if you do not like something in your life, you are responsible for changing it. If you need a break or an opportunity, you create it. Many people wait around for that golden opportunity, which rarely comes. There is one opportunity we have every day: the opportunity to do something for someone else, to be of service to mankind. And it does not matter whether we are confined to a hospital bed, locked in a prison, or working 70 hours a week.

The third key to a fulfilling life is to recognize that all limits are imaginary walls built by finite minds. The universe is yours if you will but ask for it. *There are no excuses.* When you choose, you can: create wealth, create a healthy body, become a leader of leaders, be the expert in your chosen field, discover new fields, lend a hand to mankind. You can do these things and anything else you can imagine. You can face every problem and hardship and come out the winner. You can look at the darkest storm and see through it to the bright sunlight. There are no limits.

There is no problem conceived that man cannot solve.
~ Dr. Samuel Johnson

To play with a win-win strategy is the fourth key to growth and fulfillment. In the past we were told to "practice the golden rule." Treat others with fairness as we would like to be treated ourselves. When we understand the Law of Individualization - all are one - then there's no choice. To harm another is to harm yourself. How could we justify making another human suffer, experience financial ruin or loss? It does not matter their color, their race, their nationality or social standing; *they are you.*

There is only one way to serve yourself and that is to serve others. This is the fifth key to the life we all seek. The greatest service one can give is to do all one can to raise the vibration of mankind. Each person must look within to find the best means available to achieve this great goal. PSI was created from such a desire. Many years ago we pledged to make PSI the most effective vehicle to serve mankind that we could create.

A life based on these five keys service, win-win strategies, expanded limits, personal responsibility and results is a life of peace, love, joy and liberty.

PSI has room for all those who truly desire to become a part of it. There are many ways to be a part it. Just living a PSI way of life is being a part, so is telling a friend, or donating to PSI WORLD, or helping one of our service projects. Aiding, building and teaching seminars are also available to those motivated in that direction. In fact, there are as many ways to be a part of PSI as there are individuals.

Students eagerly ask, "What is the next class I can take? Where do I go from here? What do I study next?" If you are still seeking the answers to your questions and problems in a class or a teacher or a book, you have missed the point. The answer is not outside; it is within. You already have the answers to your own questions and solutions to your own problems. In fact, too heavy a reliance on classes, books or teachers can be detrimental. They keep you from doing the one thing you must do, which is to make permanent mental changes. To be successful, you must change your thought pattern from what it is now to that of success. *To keep looking for the answer is to affirm that you have not made the change.*

It is very easy to change your thoughts for a short period of time. It happens all the time in classes, workshops and meetings. The positive atmosphere around you, an instructor reaffirming the Truths and people supporting your new ideas make it easy. You say, "I will meditate for half an hour in the morning and evening each day. I will practice the win-win strategy. I will serve my fellows." Then you go home, to school, back to the office and back into an atmosphere of negativity and competition. Five days later you are meditating only once a day for half an hour and your service is relegated to the weekends. Five months later you are not even doing that. At about this point, the thought may occur to you that you need another class. You don't really. All you need is to put the last one into action again. You had it for a moment, but you did not hang onto it. *The trouble is not in changing thoughts but in keeping thoughts changed.*

What we need to do is to keep the thoughts and attitudes the same as the day we finished that last class. Each morning when I wake up, I like to imagine that the class was just yesterday. Positive thoughts and warm feelings flood into my consciousness. I feel revived, refreshed and ready to get on with it. Yesterday was the class.

Making "yesterday the class" creates a trigger device for an uplifted mental attitude. It starts a free-flowing stream of positive thoughts, feelings and images, which carry on throughout the day. My thoughts are now concentrated on the positive, not through will power, which would be hard work, but rather through replacement. This is the way to maintain a steady and permanent thought change.

For every problem or situation you desire to change, create a trigger device to stimulate the positive equivalent. For example, suppose your problem is one of poverty. You may have spent hundreds, even thousands of hours thinking about lack and what you would do if only you had the money. Remember, wishful thinking is a reaffirmation of the problem.

The positive equivalent to a poverty-thought attitude is an abundance thought attitude. Thus, the task is to replace poverty thoughts *permanently* with abundance thoughts. Visualizing yourself in abundance is a start and could be used as a trigger device. Do not expect, however, that visualizing ten minutes or even twenty minutes a day is going to do it. What we want to create is a constant, steady stream of abundance thoughts. Look around right now. There is an abundance of stimulating books to read, an abundance of interesting people to learn from, an abundance of entertainment (TV, parks, games), many of which are available for free, an abundance of help programs, an abundance of jobs, an abundance of money - just add up the salaries of those jobs in the want ads. When you can see the abundance around you, you will then be able to see the opportunities to partake of that abundance. To think is to create. To think abundance is to create abundance - but it must be a permanent, steady thought pattern.

How great can you be? Think about this for a moment, and then answer the questions below. Answer them realistically with your true feelings. Only you will see the answers. Write your answers here, on this very page, so that you will have a permanent record of them. Turn back to this page every day if need be, to remind yourself of who you are and what you can do.

HOW MUCH MONEY CAN YOU EARN A YEAR?

HOW SOON CAN YOU GET YOUR BODY INTO GOOD CONDITION?

WITH HOW MANY PEOPLE CAN YOU EASILY COMMUNICATE?

HOW HIGH CAN YOU RISE IN YOUR COMPANY? (OR IF SELF-EMPLOYED, HOW BIG CAN YOUR COMPANY BECOME?)

HOW LONG WILL IT TAKE FOR YOU TO BECOME THE EXPERT IN YOUR FIELD?

HOW SOON WILL YOU ACHIEVE LIBERTY?

WHAT IS THE GREATEST SERVICE YOU CAN GIVE TO MANKIND?

WHAT IS YOUR HEART'S DESIRE, THE ONE THING YOU PERSONALLY DESIRE MOST IN THE WORLD?

DATES COMPLETED: _____, _____,

_____, _____

Now I challenge you to be more than you say you can be. I dare you to push your limits outward. You can achieve all those things you listed above, because you can conceive of them. You *have* conceived of them. Now conceive of greater things. Do more, be more, achieve more. Double the amount you can earn a year. Cut the time you listed to get your body in shape by a third. Triple the number of people you listed as an answer to question three. Rise to the top of your company, and double its size. Go back to school, to read and research in your field, or whatever it takes to become *the expert* in your field. Find a greater service to mankind. *Achieve your heart's desire.* Do you feel like changing some of your answers? Go back and do it. Go back and change those answers each time you dare to do more, to be more and to achieve more. *Be all that you can be!*

> *YOU ARE A CIRCLE WITHOUT CIRCUMFERENCE.*
> *YOU ARE INFINITE.*
> *YOU ARE ONE WITH THE UNIVERSE. YOU ARE THE*
> *UNIVERSE.*
> *YOU ARE INFINITE POWER. YOU ARE GOD.*
> *YOU ARE THE I AM. YOU ARE.*

Peace, love and liberty are already within you. Dare to claim them for your own.

SUGGESTED READINGS

Adizes, Ichak. *Corporate Lifecycles: How and Why Corporations Grow and Die and What to do about it.* Prentice Hall Press (February 7, 1990)

Bradshaw, John. *Homecoming: Reclaiming and Championing Your Inner Child.* Bantam (February 1, 1992)

Browne, Sylvia. *A Journal Of Love And Healing: Transcending Grief.* Hay House (February 1, 2001)

Hansen, Mark Victor and Canfield, Jack. *Chicken Soup for the Soul: Living your Dreams.* HCI (August 12, 2003)

Canfield, Jack, and Switzer, Janet. *The Success Principles: How to Get From Where You Are to Where You Want to Be.* Collins (December 28, 2004)

Chopra, Deepak, M.D. *The Book of Secrets: Unlocking the Hidden Dimensions of Your Life.* Harmony (September 28, 2004)

Chopra, Deepak, M.D. *The Seven Spiritual Laws of Success: A Practical Guide to the Fulfillment of Your Dreams (based on Creating Affluence).* New World Library (January 1, 1995)

Chopra, Deepak, M.D. *The Spontaneous Fulfillment of Desire: Harnessing the Infinite Power of Coincidence.* Harmony (October 21, 2003)

Eisler, Riane. *The Chalice and the Blade: Our History, Our Future* (of special reading interest for women). Harper San Francisco (September 1, 1988)

Farrell, Warren, Ph.D. *Women Can't Hear What Men Don't Say: Destroying Myths, Creating Love.* Jeremy P. Tarcher; Reprint edition (September 1, 2000)

Foundation for Inner Peace. *A Course in Miracles.* Viking Adult (March 1, 1996)

Gibran, Kahlil. *The Prophet.* Knopf (September 12, 1923)

Gray, John. *Men are from Mars, Women are from Venus: A practical guide for improving communication and getting what you want in your relationships.* Harper Collins Publishers; 1st edition (May 1, 1992)

Hay, Louise L. *Everyday Positive Thinking.* Hay House (March 1, 2004)

Hay, Louise L. *You Can Heal Your Life.* Hay House (June 1, 1985)

Houston, Jean. *A Mythic Life: Learning to Live our Greater Story* Harper San Francisco (November 20, 1996)

Houston, Jean. *Jump Time: Shaping Your Future In A World of Radical Change.* Jeremy P. Tarcher (May 1, 2000)

Houston, Jean. *The Search for the Beloved.* Jeremy P. Tarcher (June 30, 1997)

Jampolsky, Gerald G. *Love Is Letting Go of Fear.* Celestial Arts; Revised edition (September 1, 1988)

Karcher, Stephen. *I Ching: The Classic Chinese Oracle of Change - The First Complete Translation with Concordance.* Vega Books (October 1, 2002)

Keen, Sam. *Fire in the Belly* (of special reading interest for men). Bantam (March 1, 1992)

Keen, Sam. *Inward Bound.* Bantam (May 1, 1992)

Kiyosaki, Robert T. and Lechter, Sharon L. *Rich Dad, Poor Dad: What the Rich Teach Their Kids About Money--That the Poor and Middle Class Do Not!* Warner Business Books (April 1, 2000)

Maclaine, Shirley. *Going Within.* Bantam (March 1, 1990)

Maclaine, Shirley. *Out on a Limb.* Bantam (November 1, 1986)

Millman, Dan. *The Laws of Spirit: A Tale of Transformation.* H.J. Kramer (September, 2001)

Millman, Dan. *Way of the Peaceful Warrior, 20th Anniversary Edition: A Book That Changes Lives.* H.J. Kramer; 20th Anniversary Edition (September 30, 2000)

Morrissey, Mary Manin. *Building Your Field of Dreams.* Bantam (June 2, 1997)

Morrissey, Mary Manin. *New Thought: A practical spiritually.* Jeremy P. Tarcher (August 1, 2003)

Morrissey, Mary Manin. *No Less than Greatness: Finding perfect love in imperfect relationships.* Bantam (August 27, 2002)

Peale, Norman Vincent. *The Power of Positive Thinking.* Ballantine Books (August 27, 1996)

Hugh Prather, Hugh. *Notes to Myself: My Struggle to Become a Person.* Bantam (November 1, 1983)

Proctor, Bob. *You Were Born Rich.*

Ruiz, Don Miguel *The Four Agreements: A Practical Guide to Personal Freedom (A Toltec Wisdom Book)* Amber-Allen Publishing (November 1, 1997)

Talbot, Michael. *Holographic Universe.* Harper Perennial; Reprint edition (May 6, 1992)

Todeschi, Kevin J. *Edgar Cayce on Soul Mates: Unlocking the Dynamics of Soul Attraction.* A.R.E. Press (Association of Research & Enlig (February 1, 1999)

Todeschi, Kevin J. *Soul Signs: Life Seals, Aura Charts, and the Revelation.* A.R.E. Press (Association of Research & Enlig (June, 2003)

Tolle, Eckhart. *The Power of Now: A Guide to Spiritual Enlightenment.* New World Library (September 29, 2004)

Wattles, Wallace D. *Financial Success: Harnessing the Power of Creative Thought.* Destiny Books (November 1, 1981)

Wattles, Wallace D. *The Science of Getting Rich or Financial Success Through Creative Thought.* Iceni Books (January 1, 2002)

Williamson, Marianne. *A Return to Love: Reflections on the Principles of "A Course in Miracles".* Harper Paperbacks (April 24, 1996)

Williamson, Marianne. *The Gift of Change: Spiritual Guidance for a Radically New Life.* Harper San Francisco (November 1, 2004)

Williamson, Marianne. *Marianne Williamson on Transformation: Growth Is Messy, the Real You.* Harper Audio (December 1, 1996)

Zukav, Gary and Linda Francis, Linda. *The Heart of the Soul: Emotional Awareness.* Free Press; Fireside edition (August 6, 2002)

Zukav, Gary. *Thoughts From the Seat of the Soul: Meditations for Souls in Process.* Fireside (October 16, 2001)

THE CHALLENGE

(To be completed after The Life Success Course)

So you want to be more. You want to do more and to have more. I challenge you then to be the person you want to be – to do the things you want to do - to have all that you want to have. I challenge you to create more in your life.

Specifically I offer you the following seven challenges:

CHALLENGE 1:   Prove the concept "Man is paid in direct proportion to the service he renders mankind."

Time Limit: One month

Method: For 30 consecutive days, render a service to mankind for which you neither expect nor accept pay. The specific type of service or services is left for you to determine individually. You may work individually or in a Mastermind team.

Conclusion: On a daily basis keep track of the services you render. At the conclusion of the 30 days (and only then) look back and list your gains.

CHALLENGE 2: Demonstrate that "a fear confronted becomes a coward."

Time Limit: One month

Method: Make a list of your persistent fears. (For example: snakes, bugs, falling, heights, flying, being alone, etc.) From your list, select one fear that reoccurs frequently, and which if eliminated would increase your degree of liberty. It is suggested that you work with only one fear at a time. The procedure will be to research the fear, then to confront the fear in your actual experience.

Conclusion: After researching and confronting the fear, write down your feelings and what you have learned.

Examples:

Fear	Research Activities	Confronting the Fear
Snakes	Read on snakes, their habits and characteristics.	Observe snakes in a zoo or a pet store. Have someone hold a snake for you to observe.
Flying	Read on the principles of flight; tour your local airport/control tower.	Take a private flying lesson to experience yourself in control of the plane.
Staying Alone	Research crime prevention; ask your local police to help you make your home or apartment secure.	Take self-defense lessons, such as Karate or Judo; when you feel secure spend three nights alone in your home.

The above are examples only. Use all your talents, including your imagination and creativity to research and confront your specific fears.

NOTE: Do not in any way endanger yourself. To confront the fear of "being attacked," it is not necessary to "be attacked." Being prepared is sufficient.

CHALLENGE 3: Internalize the I AM concept. "You are what you know yourself to be in your heart."

Time Limit: Two months

Method: What characteristic or trait do you wish to further develop? Make a list then select one trait to use in this challenge.

Conclusion: Keep a "feeling" diary as you do this challenge to record what you are experiencing.
For the selected trait:

1) List those activities or appearances which represent that trait to you.
2) Take the necessary actions to cause that trait to appear in your life.
3) Maintain these actions for two months.

Examples:

I AM Trait	Description	Action
Attractive	Modern hairstyle; stylish clothes; physically fit	Join a gym/fitness group; jog mornings/evenings; buy 2 or 3 stylish new outfits; have hair styled by a professional.
Creative	Painting; writing; music; crafts	Take a class in painting or crafts; begin music lessons; keep a notebook of ideas.

The above are ideas to get you started. Be creative and imaginative in selecting the actions to create your trait. Use the screen of the mind, meditation and affirmations just might be helpful!

CHALLENGE 4:   Put words into action. Demonstrate the concept, "If you don't like something, change it."

Time Limit: One to six months

Method: Make a list of "actions" you feel need to be taken at home, work, school, or in the community. Select one in which you have strong feelings, and then take the responsibility to see it gets done.

Examples:

HOME	Outside painting/maintenance of home
WORK	Create a more positive atmosphere
COMMUNITY	See that the school crossing near your home is better marked or manned.

The above examples are just to stimulate thoughts. The screen of the mind is an excellent tool for use with this challenge.

CHALLENGE 5:   Understand the meaning of SUPPORT.

Time Limit: One month

Method: Select an organization or group in whose goal or
                cause you truly believe. For 30 consecutive days,
                totally support that group by all the means available
                to you: emotionally, with work/help, with
                knowledge, with money, with ideas, and with
                energy. Use your creative and imaginative abilities
                to make a total commitment for these 30 days.

Conclusion: Keep a log of your daily support activities. At the
                end of the 30 days (and only at the end) note how
                you feel, and answer these questions:
                (1) Could I have given more support?
                (2) If so, why didn't I?

CHALLENGE 6: Demonstrate "Balance is the key to power."

Time Limit: One month

Method: To create balance, strengthen your "weak" horse. Below are listed challenges to strengthen Pale, Red and Black Horses. Do the two which you need to strengthen (i.e., if you are a Pale Horse, then do the Red and the Black.)

Characteristics:

PALE HORSE:	To strengthen the Pale Horse is to build consciousness in the physical plane: health, physical fitness and wealth consciousness. (a) Plan and follow a 30-day health/physical fitness program. (b) Attend a seminar on investments, such as diamonds, stocks and bonds, or real estate. (Note: Such seminars are often free or very low cost.)
RED HORSE:	To strengthen the Red Horse is to follow intuition and emotions. For the next month, plan and create, at least once a week, a childlike, fun outing (examples: a picnic, kite-flying, boating, horseback riding, etc.). Invite people with whom you FEEL most comfortable to join you. Be creative and do things out of your ordinary routine.
BLACK HORSE:	To strengthen the Black Horse is to strengthen the intellect. Select one of these areas, or a similar area: history, music, art, literature, theatre, antiques. Then (a) read a book on this subject or related to this subject, and (b) twice visit a museum/gallery or attend the theatre/concert.

CHALLENGE 7: Demonstrate the validity of these concepts: "Thoughts are things" and "To think is to create."

Time Limit: Two months

Method: What would you like to create? A different place to live, a new car, a vacation weekend, better personal relationships, a more exciting job, new furniture or clothes? Select and write down one specific short-term goal. Then write down all you can envision about your goal. Finally, make a "to do" list of specific actions you can take to work toward the creation of your goal. Remember to include The Basic and Life Success Course techniques among your "to do's." Examples:

Area:	A new car	Better relationships
Specific Goal:	A new car by September 5th.	Make 3 new friends by the end of this month.
Details:	Red with white interior; automatic transmission; white sidewalls; Lincoln Continental.	Find people with whom I feel comfortable and can call to come over or do something on a moment's notice; share many likes in common.
To Do List:	See the car in the showroom. Test-drive it (be sure it is exactly as you desire). Determine cost and the financial options available (time payment, lease, rental, etc.). Check trade-in and selling options for your current car. Check maintenance and gas costs for new car; com-pare to current car. Determine total monthly cost for new car. Determine what income you will need in order to "afford" your car.	Sign up for and attend a new interest group (e.g., ski club, judo class, craft class, etc.) Invite one new person over for dinner or out to lunch or to attend the theatre or concert as your guest. Have a "bring a friend" party where each guest brings a friend to dinner, bridge, chess, wine-tasting, etc. Take on a volunteer project (you could start Challenge 1 if you have not already done it).